THE ULTIMATE BEGINNERS GUIDE TO UNDERSTANDING NFTS

LEARN HOW TO MAKE MONEY BY CREATING, BUYING AND SELLING WITH NON-FUNGIBLE TOKENS (NFTS), CRYPTOART AND BLOCKCHAIN TECHNOLOGY

LM ANDERSON

CONTENTS

ABOUT THE AUTHOR

For about five years now, I've been studying crypto and the world of NFTs. At first, I was just curious, like I think many people were about this strange new technology that was gaining momentum. But, that curiosity quickly became an obsession, and ever since I bought my first bitcoin, there's been no turning back. I love investing and technology, and the blockchain made those two passions merge into one in every sense of the word.

I'm a trader and investor at heart, and I've always looked for new opportunities in investing. I've jumped on opportunities that have been both good and bad. It's the nature of the job. The point is trying and taking risks because sometimes they pay off. I took a gamble on crypto, and it's still paying off to this day!

I wrote this book because while I love trading and investing, I have a greater passion for sharing my love and knowledge with others. Hopefully, inspiring them to take some risks of their own. I want everyone to understand the complex, and at times confusing, world of blockchains, crypto, and NFTs. Why? Because I genuinely believe that it's the future of investing, technology, and business. I think whether we like it or not, it's here to stay. So I don't want anyone to get left behind.

I'm deeply invested in this topic, and I think soon you will be too!

INTRODUCTION

If you've ever flipped on the television and seen the popular series *Pawn Stars,* you might have noticed how much money seemingly unremarkable items can get snapped up for in a heated exchange. For some people, these things might not seem all that worth the amount of money they're going for by the end of the deal. A painting bought for $390,000 or a Chinese bamboo brush pot for $470,000 to some these items aren't exciting, but to others, they're collectibles.

There's a reason why they're so sought out. Collectibles have primarily become an investment. 'A collectible is anything that can be sold for more money than it was originally worth.' *(Beattie, 2022)*. When these items were initially created, you can be sure they weren't sold for hundreds of thousands, or in some cases, millions of dollars. With every passing year, these items became rarer as production on these items ceased, and they were lost to history. However, people hung on to these items, passing them down through generations or trading and selling them to other people, and eventually, they became valuable.

What influences the price of collectibles?

The price of these collectibles comes down to a series of factors;

- **They're rare.**

The more widespread an item is, the less value it has overall. It's a common supply and demand type of situation. Consider a vintage copy of the original Godfather screenplay versus a DVD of the Godfather. One is incredibly rare and therefore extremely valuable. The other is a DVD available pretty much everywhere. In combination with the decline of physical media, it's another reason why its value is non-existent.

- **Their age.**

Older is usually better. Think of the value of a fossil from the Jurassic age or an artifact from the earliest civilizations. These items have the combination of age and place in history that help influence the amount of money they can fetch at an auction.

- **Their place of origin.**

Certain moments or places throughout history have undeniably been dubbed as more valuable than others. Some don't really care about artifacts from the time of Neanderthals but are obsessed with the Roman Empire. Different people will find different niches to occupy, and it depends on their perspectives of what is more important to them in the history of our world.

- **Their popularity.**

Some items like sneakers and toys have a great deal of popularity and novelty attached to them. This helps create a demand for items that may have been part of a limited run or were extremely popular in their time. Therefore, they now have a nostalgic element attached to them.

- **Their condition.**

This should be a given, but the better the condition of the antique/collectible, the more value it has to a buyer. Even if an item is in perfect condition, it's vital to see if the item has, in fact, been refurbished and how that refurbishing job affects the overall value.

The most successful collectible items are stamps, toys, fine art, rare coins, and sneakers *(A. Rhiannon, 2021)*. The price of a collectible is never easy to predict, thanks to the combination of these factors. So why do people even want collectibles? What is in it for them? Are there any pros and cons to investing in collectible items?

Pros of Investing in Collectible Items

There are several pros attached to investing in collectible items *(Chen, 2022)*;

- The potential for further appreciation over time.
- An item or items which can be passed down to future generations.
- The ability to collect things you're passionate about.
- The benefits of diversification.

Cons of Investing in Collectible Items

There are naturally several cons attached to investing in collectible items *(Chen, 2022)*;

- The volatility of collectibles value.
- The insane transaction fees, storage costs, and handling fees. Be prepared for these numbers.
- The unfortunate reality is that buying a fake is very possible.
- Collectibles aren't income-generating assets.

How does any of this relate to NFTs?

Knowing what you know now about collectibles, it's time to link the concept with a new type of collectibles; NFTs.

NFTs have become a global sensation. It shares many characteristics of the common practice of investing in collectible items instead this time, it's in the digital space. Suppose you think this isn't a serious market. In that case, you're clearly unfamiliar with the numbers attached to NFTs that people are ready and willing to pay.

One of the earliest NFTs to exist, known as CryptoKitties, has generated 56 million dollars in sales since it was first launched in 2019 *(Non-fungible.com, 2022)*. NFT collectible CryptoPunks averaged 2 million dollars in sales a day since mid-2021 *(Statista, 2022)*. There's an insatiable appetite for NFTs, and it's only growing. The largest NFT sale in recorded history is Pak's 'The Merge' which sold on the 2nd of December 2021 for 91.8 million dollars *(Adams, 2021)*.

Everyone is finding themselves getting more familiar with NFTs by the day, including some of the biggest celebrities in the world. Justin Bieber has added a vast number of minted NFTs to his collection. Athletes like Stephen Currey and Lionel Messi have their own NFTs that are up for grabs. More recently, Snoop Dogg announced his own collection of NFTs, which would be like a collection of art representing moments from his life with quotes from the legend himself.

The road to understanding NFTs

In this book, we're going to break down the core concepts of this new type of collectible and how you can easily navigate a whole new world of investment and opportunity. Of course, we all know the pure basics of NFTs, but very few people have taken the time to explain what they actually are and how they work.

We will explore the hype and history surrounding NFTs, explain the blockchain, understand the rise of cryptoart before we embark on a journey of understanding how we can navigate this brand new world of collectibles while knowing its limitations and common pitfalls. By the end, you'll not only know how to buy and sell NFTs, but you'll also know how to make NFTs of your own to sell. This is more than a movement, and it's time to ensure you don't get left behind.

1

NFTS - HYPE OR LEGIT?

NFTs ARE by no means new, but they're only recently exploding in terms of popularity. As a result of this growing popularity, many people are jumping headfirst into this strange yet wonderful world of revolutionized collectibles. Still, they don't really understand what this world truly is at its core.

In this chapter, we will be exploring the basics of NFTs. What are they? What's their history? How did they become so popular? What is their purpose? Are they worth the hype? Are they actually legit?

It all begins at the burning question we've all got, what on earth is an NFT?

What exactly are NFTs?

To understand NFTs, you also need to understand the world of collectibles. But, before we truly dive into that, let's just cover some basics. For starters, let's break down what NFT actually stands for; non-fungible token.

NFTs are digital assets that act as representations of things we'd find in everyday life, such as; art, videos, music, and even in-game items. The novelty behind an NFT is that they are unique, one-of-a-kind, and are sold online. The most common method of acquiring an NFT is purchasing one on the various marketplaces using cryptocurrency.

A surprising fact that you might not know is that NFTs have been around since 2014. They have become this global phenomenon that people are taking far more seriously and spending money - a ton of money on in the process. In 2021 the money spent on NFTs ballooned to over $22 billion (Howcroft, 2022). Yes, billion, with a b.

NFTs exist on a blockchain and remain there for their entire existence. There's no altering, removing, or replacing these digital assets; what you purchase and sell is unable to be changed and remains safely secured on the highly secure blockchain. But we'll dive deeper into the blockchain in *Chapter 2*. So, for now, let's focus on NFTs themselves.

What is Non-Fungible Versus Fungible

Fungibility is the ability a good or asset holds to be interchangeable with other assets or goods of similar type and value. These are meant to simplify the trade or exchange processes. So when something is fungible, it can be readily exchanged for another item or asset of like kind. However, when something is non-fungible, it essentially means the complete opposite. An item isn't able to be changed; therefore, its value can't be determined on a one-for-one system.

Consider it like this; if you borrow your friend's car and use up all the gas already in the car, you can replace the gas with the same kind of gas. However, you can't return a different vehicle, regardless of whether it's identical in every aspect. The car owner will not question a gas refill, but they won't agree that the car's value is the same if you replace it with an identical vehicle. There are things about their vehicle, which you borrowed, that don't exist in this other car. Maybe the previous car didn't have a scratch, something faulty, missing upgrades the other vehicle had, etc. There's a clear difference between these two things, one of which is fungible, gas, and one which is non-fungible, the car.

What Do You Get When You Buy An NFT?

There are a lot of things that are minted into NFTs. These digital assets represent tangible and intangible items such as;

- Art
- Music
- GIFs
- Videos and sports highlights
- Collectibles
- Designer sneakers
- Virtual avatars and video game skins

The thing is, anything can become an NFT. For example, tweets. One tweet sold for over $2.9 million, and that tweet happened to be the first-ever tweet that Twitter ever saw from its co-founder Jack Dorsey (Conti, 2022).

When you buy an NFT, you get exclusive ownership rights. This is because an NFT can only have one owner at a time. Thanks to the blockchain and NFTs unique data, ownership is easily verifiable and straightforward to transfer between owners well facilitated. Some artists even include their signature in an NFTs metadata.

How Are NFTs Used?

Do you remember being a kid in the late 90s and early 2000s? The movies had exhaustive campaigns marketing their feature films for kids around that time. In doing so, they released toys, merchandise, and more to hype the movie's release.

Years later, these products became rarer. But some of these movies not only retained their popularity, they potentially became more popular than before, gaining a cult following. As a result, some people frantically searched for all the merchandise possible. For example, consider the movie Toy Story 2, where the movie's main antagonist is obsessed with a television series based on the famous toy cowboy, Woody. He's collected some of the rarest finds of this long-forgotten series, and they're worth a lot. This is an NFT in its traditional form; NFTs are collectibles. They're digital representations of digital collectibles and other digital assets. They represent anything from artwork to licenses and even land.

. . .

This allows an avenue for artists to make money without the reliance on galleries. It's totally revolutionized the industry. They can now sell directly to consumers and negate the entire third-party system that's long been a barrier for artists. Even more incredible is that artists can set up royalties so that every time their art is resold, which means they're continuously making money on their art for its entire lifetime.

Art is obviously not the only way to make money, but it's become one of the most prominent ways thus far. Some other great examples are NBA highlight of LeBron James, which fetched a staggering $200 million, or the recent ventures by Lindsay Lohan and Snoop Dogg, who are selling off NFTs of unique memories, artwork, and moments.

Anything that is unique in form can be turned into and considered an NFT on the blockchain. NFTs are representations of not only actual assets but also, and in some cases more importantly, as ownership. NFTs are artworks, online content, music, video, real estate, loans, smart contracts, and so much more. They're used to offer a good for a price, but more importantly, they are there to provide accurate ownership information that's extremely verifiable and secure.

Main benefits of NFTs

There are many benefits to NFTs. Some of the most important benefits include things such as ownership, authenticity, transferability, transparency, and security. Let's take a look at these and a few other benefits individually for a moment to understand why they're considered such a benefit.

- **Ownership** and the proof of ownership attached to it is one of NFTs strongest advantages. These assets are indivisible, and there are protections against fakes.
- **Authenticity** is a major advantage considering NFTs are unique with a unique set of records attached to them. This allows them to gain value and the right of owners to determine how many exist on the blockchain. Since they're immune to any forms of modifications, removal, or downright replacement, it means they have an authenticity value appreciated by other unique collectibles.
- **Transferability** is incredibly easy with NFTs. They are tradable peer-to-peer in particular markets.
- **Transparency** is a benefit of the blockchain in general. Therefore, NFTs benefit from it, too, considering their existence on the blockchain.
- **Security** is another blockchain benefit, as is transparency. Blockchain provides space for secure transactions and information storage while providing a level of transparency unheard of in finance.
- **Economic Opportunity,** anyone can get in on the NFT trade. This has opened doors for people around the world to enjoy the economic opportunity and benefits of NFTs and the blockchain as a whole. As our world continues to shift, this might be a glimpse at the future of human interactions with the online world and how everyone might enrich themselves further by embracing it instead of turning away from it.
- **Inclusivity Growth** is present with NFTs as creatives from across a wide range of professions and art forms are able to come together to a marketplace and sell off their creations. Creators are getting value from their work and are able to interact with the consumer directly. Buyers enjoy an option of liquidity in various types of

assets. NFTs promote inclusive growth instead of the more isolated growth we've historically experienced.

Types of NFTs

We are used to thinking of NFTs as digital assets mainly relating to art, but NFTs actually exist in a variety of different ways that well extend beyond just art. Here are some of the different types of NFTs.

- **Collectibles**

When online collectibles CryptoKitties launched, it became the first true instance of NFTs. In 2017 these digital assets were so popular that the Ethereum blockchain network was congested. Thus it gave rise to a growing interest in this new digital collectible format.

- **Artwork**

Art has been one of the most prominent players in the NFT space. Programmable art is a blend of creativity and technology, and tons of limited edition art pieces were born from this NFT rise that is now in circulation on the Ethereum blockchain.

- **Memberships**

NFTs have also found use in the membership market, with special offers being given to people to purchase using Ether on the Ethereum blockchain in the form of NFTs. This can be anything from gaining access to unique services, limited-edition items, and products or the ability to attend special events. Because all memberships are held in one wallet, you've got a way to keep track of them all effortlessly. Furthermore, you've got the ability to sell and trade them easily on the blockchain for other assets.

- **P2E (Play To Earn)**

Imagine getting paid to play a game. Well, these are becoming more common than you think. Think of games like Axie Infinity which you can make money playing by investing and spending time in this world. This has become a (excuse the pun) game-changer. You're paid in cryptocurrency and can exchange it for real money. It's revolutionary for the gaming industry and is quickly adopted by other developers.

- **In-Game Items**

This quickly became a common choice for NFTs. In-game items are purchasable items you can access in-game. Playing a game with elements only available to the highest bidder makes the NFT more valuable and improves the longevity of the game. This is because NFTs that act as in-game items increase a game's value for players. The game developers or random creators of these in-game assets can create NFTs for games and earn royalties for these items every time they're sold.

- **Music & Media**

Music and media are beginning to experiment more and more with the blockchain and NFTs. Rarible and Mintbase are the two most prominent platforms for artists to mint their songs. Linking their music or media files to an NFT gives people the chance to outright claim ownership of these files. It's a sense of exclusivity and true connection a fan has to an artist, and it's proving popular even in its early days.

- **Coupons**

We all know what a coupon is and so the idea of NFTs incorporating this practice into their system makes sense. NFT coupons can be stored in your wallet, used, sold, or traded. Thanks to coupons and the transparency aspect of the blockchain, companies have more visibility, and with the use of Smart Contracts, they can be deactivated automatically if they expire.

- **Tickets**

NFTs are even being used to sell tickets to events. This is a secure way to purchase tickets, verify identity for an event, and store them securely in your wallet. Event organizers are now adopting this practice of setting aside a certain number of tickets and selling them exclusively on the blockchain. It's still relatively new, but it's growing in popularity.

- **Contracts & Loans**

Imagine getting a loan without the use of a bank. Well, thanks to Ethereum and the creation of NFTs, this is becoming a realistic option more and more every day. No paperwork, more ironclad agreements thanks to Smart Contracts, and far fewer fees make this one of the most beneficial uses of NFTs for people looking to engage in peer-to-peer lending. In addition, some instances of NFT loans even allow for the use of NFTs as collateral, making it far more trustworthy than traditional lending practices.

- **Real-World Assets**

NFTs can act as deeds for real-world assets. This means you pay for everything on the blockchain and then have the deed stored in your digital wallet. It can be anything from real estate to luxury goods. This maximizes the potential of cryptographic proof of ownership.

A brief history of NFTs

It's hard to argue that 2021 really propelled NFTs into our everyday lives. Most people had never heard of an NFT before 2021, but over 2020 the groundwork was laid to set up NFTs as the next global phenomenon. In 2021 we saw that playing out in real-time.

The funny thing about NFTs is that they're not as new as we think. Their history dates back to the early 2010s. So while we might believe they've just appeared out of nowhere, their history tells a far more complex story.

- **Colored Coins, 2012 - 2013**

Before NFTs were massive with the Ethereum blockchain, they were primarily on Bitcoin, before Ethereum was even a thing. In 2012, a mathematician by the name of Meni Rosenfeld introduced the concept of 'colored coins.' These colored coins would be issued and distributed on the bitcoin blockchain and comprise small bitcoins denominations. They'd be able to be as small as a single satoshi and could be used on a variety of assets, including;

1. Property
2. Company shares
3. The ability to create and issue your own cryptocurrency
4. Access tokens
5. Coupons

6. Digital collectibles
7. Subscriptions

Colored coins were shining examples of the potential that bitcoin possessed as well as an example of its capabilities. The major downside of colored coins was that in a system that didn't allow for fixed prices, it meant that colored coins' true value would be based on a number accepted by everyone. For example, if four people who are shareholders of a company agree that 200 colored coins represent 50 shares, but then one decides he's not in favor of this anymore, the system collapses.

The flaws that colored coins expressed were obvious. The point behind them is ultimately irrelevant as they opened a door that would eventually be used by NFTs to launch. While it was apparent that the potential for real-world assets existing on distributed ledgers was very possible, there needed to be a malleable blockchain to facilitate this revolutionary concept.

- **Counterparty, 2014**

While the consensus surrounding issuing assets on blockchain had propelled forward thanks to colored coins, there was an understanding that Bitcoin was not going to be the place where this was possible. So in 2014, Evan Wagner, Adam Krellenstein, and Robert Dermondy founded Counterparty.

Counterparty was built on top of the Bitcoin blockchain, designed to be the ultimate peer-to-peer financial and distribution platform with an open-source internet protocol.

Anyone was able to create assets and engage in a decentralized exchange. This would soon begin expanding over the coming years.

- **Spells of Genis, 2015**

In 2015, in Counterparty's early days, the creators of the popular game *Spells of Genesis* began issuing in-game assets onto the blockchain. They were also the first to launch an Initial Coin Offering (ICO), which at the time didn't have a dedicated name and was instead referred to as crowdfunding. Through the use of a token they called BitCrystals and used as an in-game currency, they were able to fund development projects for years to come.

- **Trading Cards, 2016**

In 2016, things were changing. Force of Will, a popular trading card game, partnered with Counterparty and launched their numerous high-profile franchise trading cards on Counterparty. These trading cards weren't unknowns; they were the likes of Pokemon, Yu-Gi-Oh, and the ever-popular card game Magic. The company went on to rank 4th in card games in North America. This risky move and subsequent success made others realize there was potential in the space for them to enjoy. In addition, they saw there was a noticeable value in having assets on a blockchain.

- **Rare Pepes, 2016**

NFTs and the blockchain itself really began flexing some staying power when memes entered the conversation. They began appearing on the platform in 2016, and one in particular really got the ball rolling; a Pepe the Frog meme collection known as Rare Pepes.

This high-profile meme frog was one of the most popular memes at the time. As Ethereum was rising in popularity, the founders of Portion, Jason Rosenstein and Louis Parker ran an auction for the Rare Pepe collection. This was a first-of-its-kind event. This is credited as being the birth of CryptoArt as the Rare Pepe wallet proved that anybody could do this. It also allowed the artist to have their art at an intrinsic value.

- **CryptoPunks and CryptoKitties, 2017**

By 2017, riding on the success of Rare Pepes and the Force of Will trading cards, Matt Hall and John Watkinson, who owned and created Larva Labs, decided it was their turn. They designed and created unique characters, which they generated on the Ethereum blockchain. This project was named CryptoPunks and would feature characters that were 100% unique, no two characters would be the same in any way, and they'd be limited to 10,000.

This CryptoPunks development led to the creation of the Ethereum token ERC721, which was designed to be the standard for NFTs on Ethereum. It tracked ownership movements, all from a single smart contract.

. . .

This revolution in Ethereum tokens and the release of ERC721 lured in CryptoKitties, a blockchain-based virtual game. The concept was to adopt, take care of, breed, and trade digital cats. It's like Tomogaci but with higher financial stakes attached to it.

CryptoKitties was a massive hit. They were discussed all over the news, the internet, and amongst crypto and blockchain enthusiasts. The Canadian-based company behind the CryptoKitties concept, Axiom Zen, overnight saw their status and image take off.

While CryptoPunks opened the door, CryptoKitties truly ran in and disrupted an already disrupted developing online world.

- **NFT Gaming, 2018 - 2020**

With NFTs becoming more known during this period, the NFT gaming and metaverse interest began to explode. Decentraland (MANA) became the first decentralized Ethereum-based VR platform. This game allowed for exploration, the ability to build, collect items, play games, and more. It's been compared to Minecraft, with the unique difference being complete ownership of the things you build, find, earn, or purchase.

Other games eventually popped up, with the likes of Enjin Coin (ENJ) and Axie Infinity (AXS) being the most widely known examples. Axie Infinity is a blockchain trident and battle game. Enjin Coin is a game that allows players to tokenize in-game items, which was quite a feature.

- **NFT Marketplaces, 2018 - 2019**

NFT marketplaces became massive in 2018 and 2019, with the NFT ecosystem becoming far more established. It wasn't just marketplaces like Open Sea and SpareRare which were firmly established during these two pivotal years. An impressive infrastructure was created as well as a sizable market of games and collectibles. Hundreds of projects were in the pipeline and released during this time, and while the groundwork had been laid for this to be a reality, these two years were now laying their own groundwork for what was about to happen next.

- **The NFT Boom, 2021**

It feels bizarre to think that the NFT boom is so fresh in our history, but it truly is something new. New blockchains like Cardano, Tezos, Flow, Solana, and more were formed. NFT sales were skyrocketing. Everyone was talking about them, making them, purchasing them, and engaging in this new digital landscape. Demand was increasing every month and continues to do so in 2022. With Metaverse becoming even more of a reality in the coming years, NFTs are expected to continue to rise in their popularity.

While NFTs are already popular, there's significant room to grow as more of the world's massive population learns and understands this foreign concept that we forget is still relatively new. This has been a wholly experimental period in NFT history, and now the future belongs to the blockchain.

How do NFTs have value?

The value behind an NFT is determined by the type of asset that it represents on the blockchain. For example, if the asset is tangible, such as real estate, the price of the NFT would be a representation of its real-world value. On the other hand, if the asset is digital content, then the value is purely speculative. The value in this instance is instead determined by the market and the conventional wisdom of supply and demand.

Of course, understand that the creator of said NFT can set its price to whatever they want. The artist usually considers the price of a digital asset, who determines what they believe its value is and what he believes a buyer's wilful cost might be to align the two ideas.

You never really know what the value of an NFT with a speculative price might end up being. The speculative prices might far exceed or underwhelm estimates. Consider the Jack Dorsey original Twitter tweet. Selling for $2,9 million probably was incredibly unexpected. It just further illustrates that the limitations on an NFT don't exist when the price is speculative, and it's more determined on consumer appetite for the digital asset and what they're willing to spend on it.

When we consider an NFTs value we use the equation: Utility + Ownership History + Future Value + Liquidity Premium (Chang, 2021).

. . .

The **utility** is determined by the use of the NFT on offer. For example, in-game assets can be used in-game or a concert/event ticket.

The **ownership history** matters from the original creator to every person who's owned it along the way. Imagine finding an NFT that your favorite celebrity once owned. Well, that's what's happening. Users are learning of celebrity purchases and waiting for them to trade off the NFTs so they can snap them up. The NFT creator can also mean something like was the case of Jack Dorsey's original tweet NFT. His name attached made it infinitely more valuable.

Like any collectible, the **future value** is always considered. The more time passes, the rarer something becomes, and the more someone builds a collection missing key pieces, the more an NFT grows in value.

The higher the liquidity, the higher the NFTs value. **The liquidity premium** is the ease with which it is to trade an NFT. The more buyers after the NFT, the better for the NFT itself.

Investors will each weigh these differently. They might be in it for the resale down the line, or they might be in it for collectible reasons. But, while each investor is different, these defining principles in price determination remain solidified.

Key Takeaway

NFTs are multi-use representations of real-world assets. Thanks to impressive growth, they're ballooning in popularity, and the financial returns are proving this with every transaction. Understanding an NFTs history, what it is, and its uses is one thing, but what makes an NFT unique is that the blockchain itself is unique. As a result, it's something that has revolutionized multiple markets, even if it has not yet been widely adopted.

It's time to dig a little deeper and understand the blockchain system in order for you to have a full understanding of this digital revolution we're experiencing and how you can maximize your existence in it.

2

NFTS, THE BLOCKCHAIN & CRYPTO

In the previous chapter, we broke down the basics of NFTs, what they are, their history, where their value comes from, and how seriously we should be taking them. Now, it's time to understand the force that keeps NFTs and all other forms of decentralized online activity up and running: the blockchain.

Understanding how NFTs, the blockchain, and crypto work helps us understand them as individuals and how they work seamlessly together. Of course, this system requires the other in order to thrive, and they've done so successfully thus far, but the question remains; what is the blockchain?

The Blockchain

In basic terms, blockchains are shared databases distributed among the nodes of a computer network. These databases electronically store information and have become crucial for cryptocurrency systems like Bitcoin and Dogecoin. They're also pivotal to NFTs as we're about to find out.

- **What Is Blockchain?**

Blockchain came about after the financial crisis in 2008. As life found itself disrupted by one of the worst global financial crises in nearly a century, the aftermath saw the birth of blockchain technology. This new unknown technology, developed during profound global financial ruin, blockchain and cryptocurrency, was hailed as a change to a vastly broken and corrupt system. But what is blockchain?

Blockchain is the gateway to financial innovation as it's the engine on which cryptocurrencies, and eventually NFTs, were built. However, how it operates is not how you'd expect a database to typically work. Transactions aren't stored in typical folders; instead, they're stored in 'blocks,' and as new transactions occur, they're grouped into these blocks. Each block has room for x amount of transactions. When it reaches the threshold, it's chained to previous blocks and added to the long chain of blocks containing transactions, hence the name *blockchain.*

Blocks are created by miners through the process of mining. Every block has a nonce and a hash. A nonce is a 32-bit whole number that is randomly generated when a new block is created. This creation generates a hash, a 256-bit number connected to the nonce, and starts with a bucketload of 0's. Miners use specific software that aids them in solving complex math problems, which gets them to locate the nonce that then generates the hash. They must explore the likely 4 billion possible combinations before finding the correct nonce and hash combination. When they find it, it's added to the blockchain.

. . .

As a result of this method of record-keeping, this digital ledger is organized in chronological order from the very first transaction to the most recent. If anybody wanted to, they could see a well-documented history of transactions made on the blockchain.

Blockchain doesn't exist in one place. It exists anywhere and everywhere. It requires an insane amount of computers and power to function. But, if one computer goes down, a network of computers has the data, so nothing is ever lost; the data lives on. They act as servers which are often referred to as nodes. Since no one person or organization can own and operate the blockchain, nodes act as the backbone of this system. It keeps the ledgers recording and the system operational. Nodes can be any device, unlike traditional servers.

- **How Does Blockchain Work?**

The way blockchain works is rather remarkable. The blockchain records every transaction, no matter its size. But, more importantly, the way it achieves this digital ledger of sorts makes it incredibly difficult, if not downright impossible, to hack, change, or cheat the system on which it exists. It's the digital equivalence of Fort Knox.

What makes blockchain so unique is that it's decentralized. This means that entities that exist on the blockchain are controlled by a distributed network such as a group of people and not a centralized entity such as an organization, government, or individual. It's a vastly different system than the ones that currently exist and have existed for centuries. Instead of closed doors, under-the-table dealings, blockchain, and everything that exists on it demand the utmost transparency and accountability.

As a result, the power of blockchain lies in the hands of users like you and me. This is in stark contrast to centralized banking, which is controlled by organizations, individuals, and federal governments.

The reason why blockchain is considered far more secure than a bank is that the blockchain isn't able to be hacked. Every touch point is tracked by the blockchain and logged into the database, giving it higher security measures and far fewer risks attached to it in terms of cybersecurity. Traditional systems can be hacked and have been hacked in the past.

Standard databases are malleable, which means they can be edited or amended to include or exclude certain transactions. This is not the case on the blockchain. Nothing can be removed or altered, only added. It acts as a chronological digital ledger of transactions but never leaves out any transaction and is incapable of doing so.

- **What Are The Uses Of Blockchain?**

There are countless uses for the blockchain. You might think it's all financial, but you'd be surprised just how vast the possibilities are when it comes to this revolutionary technology backed by extreme security measures.

Some of the things blockchain is used for include;

- **Cryptocurrencies**

One of the first things to exist on the blockchain was the very first cryptocurrency, Bitcoin. Since then, thousands of cryptocurrencies have been born, and it's been a sight to behold. Anybody can create a bitcoin currency; it's a limitless opportunity if handled correctly. Blockchain offers opportunities to anyone without barriers to entry, discriminative practices, intensive red tape, or gatekeeping. This is where decentralization has proven effective. It's the true definition of a free market system, and it's a glimpse into what the world can become if blockchain is given room to thrive. Judging by its implementation across multiple sectors, it seems to be heading that way.

- **Money transfers and payment processing**

Thanks to the creation of Bitcoin, cryptocurrency transfer apps are booming on app stores everywhere. If there's one space where blockchain has made a sizeable impact, it's in the financial sector. Thanks to the elimination of red tape, reduced fees due to a lack of third-party vendors, and making ledgers that operate in real-time, banks could save between $8 - $12 billion annually (Mearian, 2017).

- **Smart contracts**

Contracts and smart contracts aren't all that different at their core. The primary difference between the two is that smart contracts are enforced in real-time. How? On the blockchain. Pursuing contractual agreements on blockchain cuts out middlemen and increases accountability for all parties involved. This is simply not possible with traditional contracts, and maybe that's why these are gaining popularity. They not only save time and money, but they ensure all parties involved are complying with the agreement.

- **Internet of things**

When you hear the internet of things, you might not be familiar with the concept. It basically means to have everything connected to a network and controlled from a central device or devices. Outside of the blockchain, the internet of things remains vulnerable to attack. On the blockchain, however, this wouldn't be possible. The added benefit of transparency and incorruptibility of your tech products means they remain nothing more than 'smart' and not weapons against you and your data.

- **Personal identity security**

In 2020, it was reported that more than 47% of American's submitted complaints of identity theft and fraud (Bekker, 2021). Fraud doesn't just come from one place; it's a multitude of things such as forged documents, cybersecurity breaches, and data being stolen from users. By keeping personal information such as birth certificates, social security numbers, and other personal private information on the decentralized blockchain, we could see a dramatic drop in fraud claims.

- **Healthcare data collection and sharing**

While still in its infancy, blockchain technology in hospitals is already wielding positive results. The potential for cutting costs, getting information out faster, and streamlining procedures is working in hospitals adopting the practice. In an industry mired in excessive fees and bloated operations, this might be a way to change the way we look at healthcare entirely. Doctors and other healthcare professionals can share information almost immediately and with greater ease allowing for collaboration and the potential for saving more lives in less time.

- **Logistics and supply chain**

Supply chains are a lot weaker than we once thought they were, and the blockchain could change that entirely. A report conducted by Accenture in partnership with DHL found that in the US alone, there are over 500,000 shipping companies. This sheer number is causing poor communication and reduced transparency, both of which can be solved by blockchain. Their study found that the implementation of blockchain in logistics can increase data transparency, all thanks to a single source of data and truth. This can save time and money, but build trust in the logistics industry, which right now is lacking.

- **Transfer of ownership**

A good example of this is, in fact, NFTs, as you can purchase digital assets and have them transferred into your name as a result. Therefore, you own something on the blockchain. As previously mentioned in Chapter 1, an NFT can be anything from cryptoart, music, video, GIFs, etc. Blockchain, which is the whole reason NFTs exist in the first place, allows users to purchase these works and own them outright, which has made them a desirable investment in the last two-plus years. This market is only getting bigger, and it's showing little signs of slowing down.

. . .

However, NFTs are not the only example. There's an increasing desire to do away with complex paper trails and instead transfer real estate, land, and auto titles over the blockchain. This way, it provides transparent views of transfers and clear views of legal ownership without the daunting paper trails that often lead nowhere but more paper trails.

Crypto

For roughly a decade now, we've heard about cryptocurrencies. It all started with bitcoin, and for a long time, it wasn't common to hear of other cryptocurrencies. Since its inception, cryptocurrency has been treated as a fad, which wouldn't last. But, unsurprising to many, it's managed to survive this long, and by every available metric, it's thrived. Companies accept it as payments, people have become billionaires as a result of this unique currency, and more people are getting interested in this concept of decentralized finances now, more than ever before.

- **What Is Cryptocurrency?**

In the most basic understanding, cryptocurrency is an electronic peer-to-peer currency. It's not a physical currency that exists in your wallet, as a coin, or even on a bank card. Instead, these currencies exist on the blockchain.

The idea behind cryptocurrency, or electronic peer-to-peer currency, was an idea in the making for decades before it eventually picked up steam again in 2008. The idea behind cryptocurrencies was to fix what some perceived as a flawed system of money transactions or transfer methods.

. . .

One of the biggest flaws, mentioned repeatedly, was the involvement of banks, who acted as a middleman. This was obviously highly contentious in 2008 amidst the 08' financial crash. The fees they collected as a result of being this third-party service that facilitates transactions and the crash prompted a system that works around the traditional system using blockchain technology.

- **What Kinds Of Cryptocurrencies Exist?**

You likely know of Bitcoin, Ethereum, DogeCoin, Tether, and a smattering of others, but did you know that as of 2022, there are nearly 10,000 cryptocurrencies in existence (Hayes, 2022). That's an insane amount of cryptocurrencies, and the list is only growing as more and more people develop their own cryptocurrencies. Anyone can develop their own cryptocurrency provided they've got the time, energy, money, and expertise to pull it off.

- **Cryptocurrency Versus NFT: What's The Difference?**

While NFTs and cryptocurrency both exist on the blockchain, that does not make them one and the same.

Cryptocurrency is a decentralized system that runs on the blockchain capturing every transaction in a digital ledger. NFTs are unique one-of-a-kind assets that instead represent real-world items. NFTs are non-fungible, while cryptocurrencies are fungible. When something is fungible, it means it possesses the ability asset to readily be interchanged for something of identical value. When something is non-fungible, it doesn't possess this ability as assets aren't interchangeable such as a car and a house. These two things are not of the same value and, therefore, can't make a legitimate transaction.

In this regard, this is where the significant difference between cryptocurrencies and NFTs arises. Cryptocurrencies can be traded amongst themselves to equate the values. For example, trading x amount of Bitcoin for the equivalent in Ethereum is possible as they're both cryptocurrencies, which are fungible. However, NFTs cannot be traded amongst themselves as they are unique assets and this will lead to a loss in their individual value.

Cryptocurrency is a currency, NFTs are a representation of real-world assets. This is the major difference between these two different elements of the blockchain.

- **Public & Private Keys**

In order to secure assets, finances, and important information, digital keys are used to create certain permissions on the blockchain.

Public keys authorize receiving cryptocurrency transactions. These cryptographic codes are partnered with a public key. While anyone can send a transaction to the public key, a private key is needed to unlock it and prove you're, in fact, the owner of a said cryptocurrency that's been received via the transaction. These keys are usually addresses, which are shortened forms of your own public key. Public keys can be shared with anyone as they're only one step in a two-step process of actually getting money through crypto transactions.

. . .

Private keys are the keys nobody, but you should know. These allow for proof of ownership in order to receive and access funds sent to your pubic key, send funds to other public keys, or spend funds. Private keys can be a variety of things, but they're usually either;

1. 256 character binary codes
2. 64-digit hexadecimal codes
3. QR codes
4. Mnemonic phrases

While public keys can be generated with private keys, the opposite is virtually impossible due to a one-way 'trapdoor' feature. You can only have one private key but multiple public keys attached to the private key.

Ethereum

If you've been interested in the blockchain, NFTs, and cryptocurrencies for a while, then you're likely very aware of Ethereum. However, even if it's in the most basic of senses, Ethereum is widely known as the second most popular and used cryptocurrency available following Bitcoin.

While it's a cryptocurrency closely tied to Bitcoin in terms of use and popularity, the two aren't as similar as you might think. Designed to be more than just another store of value or medium of exchange, Ethereum is in a league of its own. What does that mean? Well, let's unpack all of this.

- **What Is Ethereum?**

In 2015, Ethereum was created by Vitalik Buterin, a programmer who realized Bitcoins limitations. It was designed to do one thing, and while it's effective at doing it, it's incapable of doing much more than that one specified task.

As a result of this discovery, he invented Ethereum, a blockchain network with a linked cryptocurrency called *ether* (ETH). As a result, Ethereum lies in a unique position of being both a tradable investment akin to other cryptocurrencies and software for developers to create new applications on.

Many have made the comparison between cell phones and app developers. In this case, the cell phone is Ethereum. The software usually produced on Ethereum is designed to make crypto easier to buy, sell, and use in a more streamlined and simplified way.

This has proven to be successful thus far with the implementation of smart contracts, direct transactions, bankless loans, and so much more. Most notably, the Ethereum blockchain has allowed for the creation of NFTs.

Non-fungible Tokens are becoming increasingly popular, and they're the direct result of Ethereum's creation. NFTs are one of many digital assets being made on Ethereum, but these Ethereum powered non-fungible tokens, are by far the most widely known and sought after in the world of blockchain and crypto.

- **Ethereum Versus Ether: What's The Difference?**

The main difference between Ethereum and Ether is that one relies on the other to exist in the first place, and their uses are different. Without Ethereum, Ether wouldn't exist. Ethereum is a blockchain network, while Ether is a cryptocurrency that exists and is exchanged on this blockchain network.

Ether is a digital currency that can be used in financial transactions, a store of value, or as an investment. These transactions are then stored on the Ethereum blockchain network.

Ethereum, as a blockchain network, holds many different purposes. From software creation to NFT collecting, Ethereum is the decentralized wild west of innovative applications and practices. People can create and host their applications on this network, create, buy, and sell NFTs and other digital assets, store personal information securely, all under the Ethereum blockchain network.

Smart Contracts are often mentioned first when it comes to Ethereum's potential. These contracts are very similar to your everyday contracts; two parties make an agreement, sign, and hopefully follow the terms of said agreement. However, with a Smart Contract, a few key difference makes them more appealing. For starters, they don't require lawyers, and once completed, the contracts, self-execute and deliver ETH to the appropriate parties. This has been one of the most effective uses of Ethereum, but as we mentioned before, it's only the beginning.

Token Types: ERC-721 & ERC-1155

When NFTs were created on the Ethereum blockchain, a set of standards were implemented to ensure this unique token had a set of requirements attached to it to make it legitimate and allow for variations in critical details such as value. This was known as ERC-721.

- **ERC-721**

The Ethereum Request for Comments 721, known more commonly as ERC-721, is an NFT standard that allows for the creation of unique digital tokens that represent valuable collectibles.

It goes deeper than the creation of an NFT, however. The ERC-721 makes it so Smart Contracts tied to the asset are unchangeable. It guarantees that what you're getting is 'one-of-a-kind' or tied to a series of collectibles totalling a certain number that's once again unchangeable. It implements this through the use of dedicated APIs tied to the smart contract.

ERC-721 has become the standard for issuing NFTs and represents unique assets that are one-of-a-kind and cannot be divided or interchanged thanks to stringent security measures that the blockchain possesses.

- **ERC-1155**

ERC-1155 is another type of NFT that's borrowed what the developers believed to be the best bits of the standards that came before this new separate standard. The purpose behind ERC-1155 was to create a standard for multi-tokens and for a smart contract to represent multiple non-fungible and fungible tokens. The other purpose behind this standard was to create a gas-efficient token contract by combining assets into one contract rather than having individual contracts for each asset.

NFTs Relationship With The Blockchain

NFTs require the blockchain to exist. However, their relationship is far more than simply hosting an NFT. The blockchain is the main mechanism that facilitates the creation and sale of NFTs.

NFTs rely on the blockchain to facilitate the sale of their digital assets in a safe manner and this is performed thanks to the blockchain's well-documented areas of expertise in security, transparency, and protection.

- **Security**

The blockchain provides a unique level of protection through the use of blocks. Blocks hold the cryptographic hash of prior blocks, transaction data, and time stamps. It makes it the most stringent identification measure to verify users' identities haven't been compromised. This level of protection is one of the blockchains' most significant achievements and is why it's being used for such sensitive transactions, record keeping, and documentation.

- **Public & Private Blockchains**

Through the use of public blockchains, anybody can access and use these blockchains to make transactions. On the other hand, private blockchains allow individuals to manage their sensitive information, access their funds, and complete transactions with low risk. Thanks to safe, tamper-proof- and transparent measures, blockchain technology remains one of the securest places on the internet.

- **Smart Contracts**

Smart contracts employ the blockchain to enforce the terms of the deal made in the smart contract automatically. This allows for greater transparency, accountability, and trust for businesses and investors. It's also what helps virtually eliminate identity theft and instances of fraud.

- **Transactions**

Transactions are safe and secure through the blockchain thanks to the use of both public and private blockchains and smart contracts. It's a low-risk environment with high-level encryption and safety measures ensuring you're safe from the dangers that exist on the internet as a whole.

Key Takeaway

The blockchain and, in turn, Ethereum itself is the foundation on which NFTs exist. They were built on these innovations with the creation of the blockchain first around 2008 and Ethereum's creation seven years later. Knowing and understanding the blockchain is part of what makes NFTs as appealing as they are. Without this imperative knowledge, you're wondering why this digital asset, which you cannot physically hold, has any value. But figuring out the blockchain and continuing to dive deeper into this world allows you to grasp why so many people, investors, developers, and creators alike flock to Ethereum to get an NFT of their own, or join in on what is a digital revolution in the making. Buying and owning an NFT isn't just having digital assets. It's finding a place in an increasingly digital world and buying into the future.

3

THE RISE OF CRYPTOART

CryptoArt has been steadily gaining ground as a pillar of NFTs and the power of the blockchain for a few years now. However, in 2021 instead of gaining ground, it began skyrocketing. While cryptoart, and NFTs at large, are a relatively new form of investment and technology, there's no underscoring its newfound value in an increasingly digital world.

Cryptoart is making some people millionaires. Examples like Beeple's $69 million artwork caused a stir and claimed headlines across the media for record-breaking prices. Numbers like this and other impressive examples define how massive this new digital art gallery already is and the potential it holds for everyone.

In this chapter, we're going to explore how NFTs gave rise to cryptoart and ultimately have revolutionized the world of art. We'll seek to understand why investors, art collectors, and the regular Joe off the street is buying into this world and getting excited doing so. But before we get into all the finer details, let's start with the most basic question.

What Is Cryptoart?

We're all aware that art comes in many different forms. Be it paintings, statues, sculptures, and anything else that results in the form of expression. Art is, at its core, subjective. Cryptoart is art in a digital form. This digital art is minted using NFT technology which generates value in the blockchain.

While cryptoart is digital art, we don't treat it any differently than physical artwork. It comes in a variety of forms such as pictures, gifs, VR dreamscapes, videos, music, and pretty much any other minted digital asset that falls under the umbrella of cryptoart.

Cryptoart benefits both the artist and the buyer of this art. Why? Well, for the artist, they're taking charge of their own work, negating the need for art galleries, setting the price themselves, and making money off every transaction. People who purchase crypto art get guarantees of authenticity, security, and the blockchain's ability to prevent falsifications and alterations.

NFTs are currently the dominant aspect of the NFT market and are only growing in popularity. It's also important to note that cryptoart can also be physical art that is tracked through the blockchain. While we mainly refer to cryptoart as literal digital art, many people benefit from selling their physical art through the blockchain. It's become an online gallery for the masses to explore and enjoy.

Collecting Cryptoart

WE have to understand something about art, and that is that it's an inherently social aspect of life. Consider this for a moment, buying cryptoart means essentially one thing, your name is attached to a digital asset that you own. However, you do not own the copyright, and this image is available online via a basic search. By that logic, you might be wondering why anyone, let alone you, would ever purchase a piece of cryptoart. But you're not considering that even owning a physical piece of art, let's say the Mona Lisa, you have the exact same situation, but you have a physical copy. But there are many identical copies out there that, while fake, bear a striking resemblance to an expensive piece of art. The value of art comes from its uniqueness, authenticity, and scarcity.

When we consider both physical and digital art, we must see where their similarities exist. For starters, art, in general, is treated as an investment before anything else.

We use art as a financial tool to explain our overall worth. While yes, that's not to diminish your love of art and reason for collecting it, we cannot ignore the reality they hold as status determinators. Cryptoart costs a lot of money in some cases and therefore exudes the same reality that physical art might.

Art is also something that we enjoy showing off, using as a conversation starter or piece. The same is true for cryptoart. As more people grow aware of this new form of art, they'll be interested in your ownership of certain pieces and might even know the pieces. We're not entirely at the level of a digital artist like Picasso or Michael Angelo, but there are some who've become household names because of their digital art.

Finally, art is decorative. As we increasingly move into an online world, things like the Metaverse will become more of a reality that we engage with on a daily basis. If there's one thing that the metaverse has room for, it's your digital art.

The key thing to understand is that art is social at the end of the day. We discuss the reasons behind it, the artist, the subject matter, the technique, and all the finer details. It's a way to connect and engage with other people. Without art, we'd be a far less advanced civilization. As we begin cohabitating in a digital world, social interaction is becoming more critical than ever. Of course, this is not the pivotal reason to buy cryptoart. Still, it's a good thing to understand and acknowledge when you begin exploring a piece of artwork of your own.

How NFTs have transformed business for artists

There's no denying that NFTs have shaken the foundations of the art world in every imaginable way. They've not only created a more accessible avenue for artists to gain a fanbase, but they've also managed to allow more artists to make a healthy living off of their work. Of course, some make far more than a living. But what's more important is that this is only scratching the surface. Here are some of the other pivotal ways NFTs are changing the game for artists.

- **Protection of Creative Work**

The internet is a digital wild west. It's difficult to truly control every aspect of it, and while countries have laws, they're sometimes insufficient when it comes to the protection of creative work of any medium.

NFTs predominantly are known for cryptoart but don't forget they can represent countless assets such as movies, concerts, sports events, tickets, and so much more. Before the blockchain, cryptocurrency, and cryptoart were around and thriving, digital artwork ownership was tricky, if not impossible.

Artists would have their digital artwork reposted countless times without gaining any credit for their work. While this happens with physical art, see souvenir Mona Lisa's and Starry Night's for reference, it's something that's stifled the digital artwork scene until cryptoart was born thanks to NFTs and the blockchain at large.

So how is it that blockchains allow for better protection of creative work? The answer lies in the idea of the blockchain: transparency. At the blockchain's core, it's a digital ledger. This ledger cannot be changed, only added to by future transactions. What happens on the blockchain remains on the blockchain forever, and anybody can see past ownership and transactions. As a result, we are able to see who created an NFT and who's owned an NFT. Never again is that artist without credit, regardless of how many transactions that particular NFT experiences.

. . .

The blockchain has given artists protections that the traditional art market has simply never been able to truly offer them.

- **CryptoArt vs. Traditional Art Galleries**

We know art galleries are designed to lure in the affluent members of society to purchase hand-selected pieces of art by snobby art dealers in an effort to connect artists and buyers alike. The downside of this is that it exists in exclusivity and barriers to entry that most artists struggle to breakthrough. Furthermore, they exclude a large portion of the population in favor of millionaires and billionaires.

Cryptoart exists on the blockchain, it's sold through numerous readily available platforms and avenues, and anybody can join, buy, and sell. NFTs completely remove that middle man mentality that exists with traditional art galleries. Instead, artists directly connect with consumers on their own terms.

The royalty system, however, is perhaps the most pivotal difference between cryptoart and traditional art galleries. When an artwork is sold at an art gallery, the artist makes their money, and that's it; it's over. That art is then resold multiple times, sometimes for more than it was originally worth because it's gone up in value. An increase in value can be attributed to a multitude of factors. For example, the artist is more famous than they were when you purchased that artwork. The owner of said artwork is high profile, and their name on the sale gives it more value. However, the artist doesn't see more money from the resale of their prized creation. They tapped out at the first sale. With cryptoart and NFTs at large, it's a bit different. Artists get a cut on every sale. Not just the first sale, or the up to a certain number of sales, all sales.

As a result of these differences, not only has cryptoart given value to artists and their work, they've proven lucrative for artists and destroyed the notion of the starving artist.

- **The Universal Benefits of Cryptoart**

Perhaps one of the greatest aspects of how cryptoart is revolutionizing the art world is its inclusivity. I've mentioned before how art has a level of exclusivity to it that has acted as a way to keep class mixing to a minimum. But NFTs have changed everything about the art world. There's no gatekeeping in cryptoart. Anybody can create, sell, or buy cryptoart. It's opened up an entire world to consumers who were previously shut out of the process. No more ultra-wealthy only clubs. Now everyone can jump into the world of art and reap the benefits of this unique industry. While yes, celebrities, corporations, organizations, and more affluent people and industries are getting into the game, that doesn't mean there's no space for the everyday Joe to exist and thrive in this world too. No more barriers to entry, no more snooty art galleries, just art and art enthusiasts existing on one blockchain together. Art is a social tool, and blockchain has proven that vision is alive and well.

NFTs and Cryptoart as Investments

For centuries, art has been purchased by the rich and powerful, and sometimes it's displayed in their homes, but more often than not, it's stored away hidden from the world, growing in value. NFTs are never hidden away from the world. Their ownership, however, is exclusive to the owner. NFTs and cryptoart are legitimate investments, and every Tom, Dick, and Harry is jumping on the bandwagon. Even more impressive are some of the massive names in the world of business, tech, entertainment, and other high-profile industries, who are also making their mark on the cryptoart world. So let's explore cryptoart as an investment.

- **Are NFTs and Cryptoart Good Investments?**

As mentioned many times before, investing in art was only exclusive to a certain subset of society. This subset was extremely concentrated, but now NFTs and cryptoart have changed much of that. If you're unsure if cryptoart is a good investment, perhaps because you view it as illegitimate art, then let me pivot your thinking.

For a while, many people may have completely agreed with the notion that NFTs were not as valuable as they were made out to be and that they were a fad. Those people have since been proven wrong. Forget about the monetary proof that is evidence that NFTs have value and are viewed as legitimate instead, let's turn to art galleries. Art galleries are now getting in on NFTs. This is not the case with all cryptoart, but some cryptoart is actually auctioned off at auction houses. This, in combination with their monetary success, proves the value of NFTs as an investment.

But are NFTs and cryptoart good investments? How do you actually make a return on your investment, and what is the potential? For starters, it's important to remember that, like art, cryptoart and NFTs are all valued differently based on a series of criteria.

. . .

Let's examine the case of Trevor Jones. Jones was a traditional artist who embraced the cryptoart scene. He released a piece titled 'EthGirl.' He released this art for only 70 Ether ($10,000 at the time). Since then, it's appreciated in value and within two years became worth a whopping $8 million. At the time of creation, NFTs weren't as hyped up as they are now. The supply and demand shift has contributed to this staggering increase in value over time. The rules of the art world aren't unique to the art world. Rarity breeds excess worth. With real-world everyday items, when the supply and demand are out of balance, we experience inflation. In the world of collectibles, we experience appreciating value due to their rarity. We govern value by these supply and demand principles across the board.

Another thing to keep in mind is that the artist who creates the artwork might not be a well-known artist at first. However, we never know the trajectory their reputation and popularity will take on. It's important to understand the artist behind the cryptoart. This might give some insight as to how the value could potentially increase over time. Considering NFTs are only expanding in influence, it's safe to say that their value and demand are only set to increase too.

Investing in cryptoart requires knowledge and the ability to study and understand the art and its history. There are so many marketplaces available, but be wary of the less reliable ones. It's best to stick to marketplaces such as OpenSea, Nifty Gateway, SuperRare, Rarible, and Foundation. To participate in this new world of investment opportunities, you need to understand what you're potentially investing in to make worthy investments.

- **High Profile Investments**

There are numerous high-profile examples of investing in NFTs and, more specifically, cryptoart. There are a host of examples of high-profile cryptoart creators like Paris Hilton, Snoop Dogg, and Lindsey Lohan. But let's focus on those specifically investing in cryptoart.

From being a Shark on Shark Tank and being one of the biggest investors in the US, Mark Cuban knows a thing or two about what to do with his money. He doesn't invest in things that aren't worth his time and money. So when he began exploring the world of crypto, he found himself understanding it and wanting to get in on the action.

While Cuban has been keeping tabs on this emerging market for a while, what really got him hooked was when he minted his own NFT. A selling point for him was the earning opportunity for royalties on every purchase of the NFT. Since then, Cuban has gone deeper and deeper into the space and has amassed a sizeable collection of NFTs and cryptoart. He's even investing in blockchain companies. Even his fellow Shark from Shark Tank, Keven O'Leary, is jumping into the world of NFTs.

Paris Hilton, as previously mentioned, has become a darling of the blockchain. She's not only making a killing selling cryptoart; she's buying it too. As a result, she's become a prominent voice in the world of NFTs, and that's lured more people in as they follow the savvy heiress into the future.

. . .

A lot of musicians realize they can cash in on NFTs to bolster their portfolios by both releasing their own or investing in existing NFTs. Popular examples include Justin Bieber, Azalea Banks, Kings of Leon, Grimes, Shawn Mendez, and many, many more.

- **Cryptoart Vs. Other NFTs Value Over Time**

Cryptoart is obviously not the only kind of NFT in existence. NFTs are the collective name for a ton of digital assets. This means that not all of them are worthwhile investments, and their investment worthiness differs from asset to asset. They also all have their own risk attached to them. The biggest risk is value. Will it appreciate in value or depreciate in value? That's the million-dollar question, literally.

Don't be scared off now, because cryptoart is far less risky than other NFT investment opportunities. Why? Simple, four reasons:

1. You know the authenticity of the artwork
2. You know the artist behind the artwork
3. You can trace the ownership thanks to the blockchains transparency measures
4. You know if it's an edition or not

Don't simply buy an NFT for fear of missing out on an NFT boom. This is what leads to risky and ill-advised investments that have the potential to depreciate in value. Also, remember that the word investment doesn't mean by and resell. You're going to be holding onto these assets for a while, so don't look to make a quick dollar. That's not how investing works.

. . .

Types of NFT investments that aren't going to count as investments are things such as event tickets which are time-sensitive. Riskier investments are real-world assets and gaming. It's all about understanding each type of NFT and assessing their risk in real-time. What makes sense, and what doesn't. What has the biggest risk of volatility, and what is more stable. These change constantly, but cryptoart has remained the steadiest of the bunch.

- **The Entertainment Value of NFTs**

Investing can be both fun and intimidating as an experience. Cryptoart, however, is one of the best entry-level investments you can make into the blockchain. It's fun and far less intimidating than cryptocurrencies and a full-on understanding of the blockchain. This is why it's so inclusive. You don't have to understand every aspect of the blockchain to participate. You can be a little more ignorant, as some of the people who actually go and purchase art from the art galleries. Not all of them are doing it because they love art sometimes. It's just about playing the game.

From this entry into the blockchain investment game, you're opening yourself up to a great deal of opportunity. This is how you will grow in the blockchain and as an investor.

- **Why Are NFTs Great Investments?**

NFTs are great investments for a series of reasons. For starters, the democratization that the blockchain has created has fostered an online community of millions. People are becoming personally invested in this concept in practice and finding new ways to push it forward to reach its full potential. It's a collaborative space in an otherwise uncollaborative reality, and that's unique.

NFT investments are great for a lot of different people too. Artists lost a lot during the pandemic, and NFTs have risen to the challenge of providing a more stable market for artists to enter without fear of world events killing their careers. Artists are thriving when before the blockchain, they lived a less hyperbolized 'starving artist' lifestyle.

Getting in on NFTs now is great timing. They're extremely popular already, but nobody is expecting this to be the piqued interest. Expectations are that millions more are still figuring it out and are slowly entering this new realm of online existence and interaction. So joining what is a 'digital revolution' means you're also engaging in the future as it's being written. It's all rather exciting. Money aside, it's an experience that comes attached to every investment and interaction on the blockchain. Those are invaluable.

- **Are NFTs Safe Investments?**

Yes, overall, they are safe, that doesn't mean there aren't safer investment opportunities out there. Investing, as a practice, is all about taking risks. You need to understand that even though NFTs like cryptoart, collectibles, etc., are worthy investments, they're still investments at the end of the day. They've got risks attached to them.

Many have predicted that NFTs would die out, that's yet to happen, but there's always that risk. Nothing is ever truly guaranteed. The same can be said about the NFT bubble, which many have predicted will burst. It's not impossible, but it's considered more or less unlikely. Once again, though, the risk exists regardless.

You, as an individual investor, need to assess the risks you're willing to take. Go big, or go home. At the end of the day, the decision lies within your digital wallet, not mine.

Key Takeaway

Cryptoart isn't the be-all and end-all of NFTs. It's a subset of a larger subset of the blockchain. However, cryptoart has emerged as a dominant market in the world of NFTs, and everyone is gaining interest in how and why this is such a massive deal. People are making and spending millions of dollars on digital art that a few years ago we may have said was the dumbest thing we'd ever heard. But, we're not laughing anymore. We're watching history being written and the future taking off.

. . .

Getting involved in NFTs doesn't take millions of dollars, it's actually easy to get started with next to nothing. So it's time to decide, are you embracing the future, or turning away from it? As you'll soon learn, getting involved in cryptoart and the blockchain at large is nowhere near as hard as you think.

4

GETTING IN ON THE ACTION

OKAY, so you're a little more understanding of what an NFT is and how the blockchain works. So what now? Well, it's time to get in on the action! That's right, in this chapter, we're going to discuss how you can start investing in NFTs. While the rich and powerful already have made headways in this department, that doesn't mean it's too late for you to join in!

You, too, can be a part of this crypto craze, but there are some things you need to know before going out and buying something. So I'm going to explain how you can invest and what to keep in mind before you start investing. This is a complex world, and you need to know what you're getting into before you start playing with the big boys and girls spending millions of dollars.

Do You Need To Be Rich To Invest In NFTs?

This is probably the most frequently asked question about getting into NFTs. I understand why many people raise the question. NFTs, from an outside perspective, might seem like a rich man's game, but that's not how the world of NFTs works at all. NFTs were always meant to be about more than just the upper-class members of society. Remember what we discussed in Chapter 3 about how NFTs democratized art and made it more accessible to all? Well, that applies to the entire NFT world. Now, that's not to say some NFTs might simply be out of reach for your budget, but it's about starting out and building a portfolio and your wealth.

Art is about having a keen eye, and let me shatter some perceptions for you right here and now. Most NFTs aren't selling for thousands or millions. They're selling for a few hundred dollars. The point is to go in looking for an investment that you deem worthy of appreciating in value over time. For example, Taco Bell released a collection of GIFs. There were 25 in total, and they each sold for about $1.60. Some of these were resold days later for $20,000. Do you see the point?

It's all about having the knowledge and conviction to make the best investments possible. It's also about trusting your gut and learning from your mistakes. Don't expect to be a pro right off the bat. You're going to make mistakes, and that's okay. What's not okay is making mistakes and not learning from them!

Why Buy NFTs & Cryptoart?

If you're still asking this question this late in the game, I'm worried. But if you're still on the fence and need some further reminding and persuasion, then I'm the guy to give it to you.

- **Exposure To The Blockchain & Cryptocurrency**

NFTs and, more importantly, the Blockchain isn't going anywhere. This is the future, and you either embrace it or risk falling behind and being kept in the dark. It's an unfortunate reality for some who might be less than keen to join the 'digital ranks.' Still, it's quickly becoming apparent this is our new reality. So, beyond a need to get exposed to this new world, you should actively want to engage in something as exciting as the blockchain. We're still in the early stages of this new technology, and the future is very much bright for blockchains, crypto and NFTs.

- **Secure, Semi-Anonymous Investments**

There's a ton of security in the blockchain, which makes investments safe and secure. You've also got the ability to store your NFTs in an autonomous digital wallet. This has been a significant aspect of the blockchain that's definitely lured people in to understand how and why this is possible. Additionally, it's been successful in keeping people's attention while keeping their money and assets safe.

- **Building a Crypto Portfolio**

It's so important to have a portfolio in order to be taken seriously in the NFT, crypto, and cryptoart space. You want to be a serious collector who's finding the hidden gems online. The more you engage in this world, the better you understand it. And from better understanding comes smarter investments! It's the circle of trading, and it takes a moment to master like pros that have been doing it for years.

- **Art Collector Without The Hassles**

This is an innovative way to be an art collector. It doesn't require all the maintenance that comes with owning a physical copy of something truly expensive. Imagine having a million-dollar painting in your home, don't think it's just going to sit on the wall, and that's it. It requires maintenance constantly. NFTs don't need that kind of attention which makes them great considering how low-maintenance they genuinely are.

- **Supporting Art & Artists**

We talk so much about making money ourselves that we forget that we're a part of a major movement bringing the power back to art and the artists. Nobody can deny that recent decades, and perhaps centuries, have really made the art world this very exclusive, and sometimes toxic, environment where money was far more valuable than the art or the artist behind the art. That's changing, and it's great to be supporting passionate artists thriving on the blockchain.

- **NFT Bonuses**

NFTs are sometimes sold with bonus content attached to them, adding a layer of exclusivity to a digital asset. It's great when you stumble upon a great find like this! So if you're a true collector, you'll surely benefit from getting content as exclusive as NFT bonus content.

What Investing In NFTs & Cryptoart Entails

Going into investing in NFTs requires a few things to ensure success. For starters, you need a healthy dose of reality. Investing in NFTs is in no way a sure-fire way to make it big, and it's going to take a moment to actually see results. Sure, some people have gotten lucky right off the bat, but not everyone experiences the same trajectory. It's also impossible to tell which way an NFT can go. It can depreciate just as easily as it could appreciate. The art world, even in its digital form, is fickle.

With that out of the way, the other thing that you need to know is the risks associated with NFTs and cryptoart investments. Of course, you're investing, it's like stocks, and stocks have risks, so this shouldn't be a surprise. But it's funny because the risk doesn't actually lie as much with the NFT as it does with what gets you that NFT: cryptocurrency.

If you know anything about cryptocurrency, you likely know that they are incredibly volatile. While, yes, they've been around for more than a decade, they're still extremely new. As a result, cryptocurrencies value can change instantly, and that change can either be modestly positive or extremely negative.

Let's say your NFT is priced in Ether, and the value of Ether drops 50%. That means your NFT just became worth 50% less as a result. This makes investing in NFTs and cryptocurrencies very similar to the stock market, where bad investments, lousy market reactions, or a combination of both can completely wipe your investments out instantly.

Beyond market volatility, it's also a guessing game. You're going in and purchasing NFTs you believe will appreciate in value. That might not always be the case. NFTs value is determined by what people are willing to spend on them, and the resale can be less than what paid for it in the first place. But, of course, that's assuming anybody even wants it.

This is why you must research things before making a commitment. Understand the risks and only spend money you're willing to potentially lose. Never over-extend yourself and find that lost investment the thing now leaving you without running water and electricity. Savvy investors don't place all their money on a long shot. It's investing, not gambling.

What Do You Get When You Pay For An NFT

When you purchase an NFT, you buy the rights to transfer the token to your digital wallet. This makes you the sole owner of the token. A token represents ownership of the original digital assets. It's the same as if you went to an auction and bought a famous painting or collectible. Only this asset you own is digital and stored in a digital wallet. You receive ownership in the form of a private crypto key, and a public crypto key.

A private crypto key is proof of ownership of the original. In contrast, a public crypto key is a certificate of authenticity for the NFT.

How To Start Investing In NFTs

Okay, so you're ready to start exploring NFT marketplaces to find an NFT that resonates with you? That's awesome! Now it's time to embark on a series of steps to make that purchase. First, let's run through each aspect of the investing journey.

- **Choosing An NFT**

The first thing you'll want to do is to start exploring some of the NFT marketplaces. Next, you need to get familiar with all the options to know where to look and what to look for.

Here are some of the most prominent NFT marketplaces:

- **OpenSea**

Leading the pack, we've got OpenSea. This free-to-sign-up platform currently dominates the NFT sales, so you'll definitely find some interesting things up for sale. It's filled with extensive offerings and supports the artists through the use of easy-to-navigate processes that help you create your own NFT.

One of its biggest strengths is that it offers more than 150 payment options. This is a great place to start if you've never seen an NFT marketplace before.

- **Rarible**

Like OpenSea, Rarible is a major player in the NFT space. It's got a wide range of NFTs, but its biggest difference and the potential downside is that it requires the use of its own token, Rarible, for sales and purchases. Rarible's worked with a ton of big brands over the years like Adobe, Taco Bell, and Yum! Brands.

- **NiftyGateway**

NiftyGateway has some heavy hitters associated with it, such as Beeple and Grimes, to name a few. Powered by the Winklevoss Twins cryptocurrency Gemini, Nifty Gateway sells NFTs built on Ethereum. It's a curated platform that stores your NFTs for you. Additionally, sales can also be made using fiat currency without the need to buy crypto first.

- **SuperRare**

SuperRare allows for NFT sales to be purchased using Ethereum and has even recently announced its own token of the same name. These tokens will put to good use looking for new emerging talent for the marketplace, making it unique in that it commissions art. Cryptoart on SuperRare can be sold on OpenSea.

- **Foundation**

Foundation is a more exclusive NFT marketplace. Artists need to receive 'upvotes' or a direct invitation from fellow creators already on the platform in order to post their own cryptoart on the platform. Because there are quite a few barriers to entry, cryptoart on Foundation is usually looked at as being higher-caliber.

- **Axie Marketplace**

Axie Marketplace is where the online video game Axie Infinity sells a ton of its in-game assets. These assets can be new characters, entire lands, etc. They're also available on various other marketplaces.

- **Larva Labs/CryptoPunks**

Larva Labs is best known for CryptoPunks, a series of NFTs given away long before the market was as hot as it is now. At the moment, they're working on new projects, but their CryptoPunks series remains incredibly viable and is fetching millions through resales. They're available on various third-party marketplaces and on Larva Labs.

- **NBA Top Shot Marketplace**

NBA was an early adopter of NFTs and has made its mark excellently on the market. You can find collectible moments such as video clips and game highlights, as well as art. This is a closed market serving only the NBA where everything is sold and traded through the platform, meaning you won't be able to sell anything from NBA Top Shot on any other marketplace.

- **Mintable**

Mintable is another marketplace with some big names behind it, with Shark Tank shark Mark Cuban even endorsing the platform. It's on a mission to be as big, if not bigger, than OpenSea. It requires Ethereum from the crypto exchange and supports the minting of all digital assets.

- **Theta Drop**

Theta Drop is a platform for the decentralized distribution of video and TV. It debuted in 2021 with the World Poker Tour's digital collectibles. The World Poker Tour was the earliest adopter of ThetaTV.

- **Open a Digital Wallet That Allows NFTs & Cryptocurrencies**

Any interest in the blockchain requires a digital wallet to hold and use cryptocurrencies. Beyond the purchasing, sending, and receiving of crypto, it's also where all the assets you purchase are accessible. So Wallets play a pivotal role in how you're able to interact with the blockchain.

I've spoken a bit about digital wallets, but I've not mentioned that there are different kinds of digital wallets. So it's not just one uniform thing, it's akin to an internet company where the purpose and access to something are the same, but the means of access are different.

When you're choosing a wallet, you need to consider the following things;

1. Security strength
2. Compatibility with numerous NFT marketplaces, especially the ones you want to use
3. Cross-device use
4. Multichain support
5. Easy-to-use and understand interfaces

Here are some of the most popular digital wallets you're going to have to consider when entering the crypto world.

- **MetaMask**

MetaMask is currently considered to be the most popular digital wallet option available. It's probably because of how easy it is to use, thanks to a handy browser extension that allows for easy accessibility to web3 sites, which is what NFT marketplaces are running on. Another popular feature is the easy ability to set up multiple addresses, so you're able to hold your crypto and NFTs separately while still having access to both seamlessly.

Another feature that's been added more recently but is extremely popular is the built-in swap feature. This allows you to swap currencies in order to buy NFTs across different marketplaces which might use different cryptocurrencies. You can limit how much you pay in gas fees. However, this does open you up to a risk of transaction failure.

- **Math Wallet**

A strong second choice behind the almighty MetaMask, Math Wallet supports more than 70 blockchains, which is insane. Like MetaMask, there's a web, desktop, and mobile app version of the wallet which seamlessly syncs across devices. Math Wallet has integrations with various hardware wallets and allows for multiple addresses.

Math Wallet also has a built-in dApp to view NFT marketplaces; it's slightly better than MetaMasks, but just barely. Finally, it allows staking, swapping and has its own utility token.

- **Alpha Wallet**

This open-source crypto wallet is good but isn't void of limitations. It's mobile-only, and even more limiting is that it's only for Ethereum. Its native support for blockchain games as well as NFTs is the reason why it stands out. Otherwise, this wallet might not be too impressive.

. . .

It has a simple-to-use interface, so beginners usually flock to this wallet. There's a whole section dedicated to gaming tokens and NFTs. You've got the ability to add meta tags to the tokens so you can make the search function work more efficiently. It's got a built-in dApp and works primarily with OpenSea, CryptoKitties, and a slew of other marketplaces.

- **Trust Wallet**

Trust Wallet is a rather popular digital wallet that's mobile-only. Owned by Binance, it supports multiple blockchains, including the popular Ethereum. Due to its Binance ownership, it is geared towards smart chain tokens.

On the more standard side of things, there's a dApp built-in and an exchange feature for swapping currencies more easily.

- **Coinbase Wallet**

Coinbase is one of the more widely known digital wallets. Most people who've just entered the space know only of Coinbase due to its immense reputation. COIN offers non-custodial wallets which are suitable for holding NFTs and other tokens.

2021 saw them releasing their own browser extension, putting them on par with MetaMask and Math Wallet. It features a built-in dApp, and the biggest advantage is the ease with which this wallet can transfer tokens to other wallets through the use of usernames and not public wallet addresses. This allows for a more personal style of transactions as well as a greater sense of security. There's also a one-click cloud backup for private keys to ensure you never lose access to your NFTs and funds.

- **Purchase Cryptocurrency To Fund Your Wallet**

The next step now that your wallet is set up is funding your wallet. To fund your digital wallet, you'll need to use fiat money to purchase cryptocurrency. Without cryptocurrency buying an NFT is extremely difficult as most marketplaces don't accept anything other than some form of crypto. When choosing which platform you're going to buy NFTs from, be sure to check which cryptocurrency they predominantly use.

- **Connect Your Wallet to An NFT Marketplace**

Now that the wallet is set up and funded, it's time to connect it to that NFT marketplace you've had your eye on. Setting up a connection between your wallet and the marketplace is relatively straightforward, and once connected, you'll be able to purchase some NFTs.

- **Buy The NFT**

It's likely you've already decided on an NFT before even setting up your wallet. But even if that's not the case, you can search for that perfect NFT to kick off your journey as a collector and investor of NFTs. Don't forget that if you're purchasing an NFT with Ethereum, you'll be required to pay a gas fee in order for the platform to process the transaction. This fee varies, but you can use services like NFT Gas Station to get a rough estimate of what it might cost you.

- **Transfer To Digital Wallet**

You bought an NFT, congratulations! Now that you're the owner of an NFT, you'll give it a moment to fulfill the transaction before you are able to view your precious NFT. The transfer into your wallet isn't complete until the blockchain network that supports the NFT has confirmed and verified the transaction. Once it's in your wallet, the transaction is considered complete. Remember, transactions can't be taken back, canceled, or reversed. It's yours until you decide to sell or trade it.

Considerations In Choosing An NFT Marketplace

By now, you've realized that the sheer number of NFT marketplaces means you're somewhat spoiled for choice. However, the critical thing to understand is that not every marketplace is worth your time. Therefore, you need to determine which ones are worth your time, and it comes down to a series of factors you need to consider.

- **Things To Check**

Here are some things you might want to consider when shopping around for online NFT marketplaces.

- **Token Standard**

The first thing you're going to want to investigate about any NFT marketplace is what token they're using. Each token has its pros and cons. These are determined by your NFT application. These are the four most common tokens used by Ethereum-powered marketplaces:

- ERC-721 = This token is the true pioneer of NFTs.

Every unit is rare and unique and is the go-to option for amassing rare collectibles.

- ERC 998 = This token is non-fungible, and users of it can compose ERC 998 tokens into complex positions and trade them on single ownership transfers. Furthermore, these tokens can hold uniform fungible units like ERC 20. Therefore, they're most recommended for people looking to hold a diver digital asset portfolio for long-term gains.
- ERC 1155 = This is the leveraging token. They allow users to leverage the same smart contract in order to hold both non-fungible and fungible tokens. ERC 1155 is perfect for NFT game collectibles like in-game exchangeable assets or fungible tokens for things like transactional currency.
- FA2 = FA2 tokens are common but not as common as some of the others mentioned above. They're equipped with unified token contract interfaces, and they support fungible, non-fungible, transferable, non-transferable, and multi-asset contracts.

- **Verification Process**

You want to find a platform that's got exceptional security, especially as more and more people become aware of NFTs, the greater the risk for scammers and hackers becomes. While the blockchain is a lot safer than other elements of the traditional internet, they're by no means impervious to con artists and thieves. This is why you want a marketplace that's got tight, strict verification processes that keep out unscrupulous users and creators.

. . .

You don't want to be in the company of unethical creators that are minting things without the original owner's permission. This is how people lose money quickly on the blockchain, and it's why people should never jump the gun on purchases. The best authentication process is a two-factor authentication process that uses either biometrics or code.

- **Price Discovery**

This is a relatively new feature, and while some platforms have quickly embraced and incorporated it into their marketplaces, many haven't. This feature is rather essential not just for sellers but buyers too. A price discovery feature helps you estimate the right rates that have the highest potential for attracting buyers. For buyers, they can use this tool to make the most informed purchasing decisions. This functionality will likely end up on all NFT marketplaces in the coming years as more and more people gain knowledge of this world and begin accessing the marketplaces, trying to get in on the action.

- **Tokens Fractionalization**

I think this is a must, but you might disagree. Look for a platform that offers token fractionalization so that you can sell NFT shards. This makes selling an NFT somewhat easier as you don't have to wait for the highest bidder; you're instead selling off pieces of an NFT. For buyers, it makes NFTs more accessible when they're high value as they can buy a piece, whereas before, they couldn't afford the NFT in its entirety.

- **Wallet Compatibility**

You don't want to be on an NFT marketplace that only works with a single or minute amount of wallets. You want to find a marketplace with a great deal of wallet compatibility to ensure it's easy for people to load up and buy NFTs. The fewer wallet choices available, the worse off buyers are as they're left without options except the option to go and find a different marketplace that will take their money. Beyond options, it should be easy to set up, seamless to use, and secure.

- **User Incentives**

There are a lot of active NFT marketplaces out there. I've even mentioned a few, but it's nowhere near all of them!

- **Always Investigate Further**

Try and see what the users of these platforms think about the marketplace before ultimately committing. Although some might be more honest than others about the marketplace's high points and low points, it's essential to determine if they're trustworthy. Some marketplaces have dubious practices, and you want to know what they are so you can be prepared or know so you can walk away.

The final thing I'll say is that marketplaces can shut down and take all your NFTs in the process. So it's best to think of using a marketplace with a well-established reputation and one that's been around more than a minute.

Storing Your NFTs

Selling and buying NFTs is one thing, but how do you store the NFTs once you've made your purchase? The first thing you need to know is that there are two types of wallets, and that's software (hot wallet) and hardware (cold wallet). Most people choose to have multiple wallets, one for daily use and one for long-term storage or protective storage measures. Software wallets are usually required by marketplaces when setting up, so pretty much everyone usually has both, even if they don't use one or the other. Cold wallets are more secure than hot wallets considering the data is stored off-chain and offline.

Beyond deciding on which wallet to use, it's important to also take NFT and crypto wallet back up into account. Having both your NFT and crypto wallet at all times, just in case something happens, is essential for both creators and buyers of NFTs. Most people use Digital Vault to ensure a copy of their NFTs exists in case of loss or accidental deletion. This is a protective measure in the event of highly trafficked NFTs that are sold and resold endlessly. Some people still use paper records for password or seed phrase backup. This is definitely not the best method of protection or backup due to potential theft or loss.

Here are some of the options you need to consider when it comes to NFT storage.

- **Software Wallets**

Software wallets are considered the standard security for NFTs. Everything that you do on your browser is encrypted and secured using a 12-24 word seed phrase and a password. Unfortunately, this is easy to hack and with the scams that are common today, it's becoming more of a liability than ever.

Hackers can easily gain access to your wallet by gaining access to the device that you use to log into your software wallet.

Another method hackers are using to gain access is getting wallet holders to give them access unknowingly by signing transaction hashes and allowing the hacker complete unfettered access to their wallets. This is incredibly common on Discord and through social media.

It's advised that you never store software wallet passwords online and always disconnect your wallet from sites before logging out of your wallet altogether.

- **InterPlanetary File System (IPFS)**

An IPFS stores NFTs off-chain and this helps to decrease the chances of being hacked. They're also considered safer and that's thanks to their content identifiers which are hashes of data connected to your NFT's content which is different from HTTP links that are vulnerable to hacks and modifications.

These hashes of data are stored on your device and searched for by the IPFS when you request data. It verifies the data by rehashing on the receiver's computer. There's still a potential for being hacked via your computer, but it's more secure than a software wallet.

- **Cold Storage Hardware Wallet**

A cold storage hardware wallet is considered the most secure option. They provide by far the most secure of all the available options. This is achieved by the system storing all your wallet data offline as well as being protected by a device password. They also have the ability to restore device content if it's been stolen or lost.

. . .

You're able to connect a cold storage hardware wallet to the internet via the device's mobile connectivity, which means you can use it as a hot wallet. They're still secure while you're connected and making transactions. The most popular cold storage hardware wallets are Trezor and Ledger.

Building An NFT Collection

Building an NFT collection takes time and shouldn't be rushed. Too many people are buying NFTs for buying NFT's sake. They're not invested in what they're purchasing. They're just buying stuff because of the craze surrounding this new market.

You want to actually be mentally invested before becoming monetarily invested in NFTs.

- **What Makes a Great NFT?**

When determining if an NFT is good or not, focus on three key factors; rarity, quality, and valuation.

Rare = You don't want to be buying NFTs that artists are to distribute infinite copies of, instead you should be aiming to focus on artists that create limited quantities of collectibles. A great example of this is the NBA, who's truly mastered the art of making quality art in limited quantities, therefore making it rare and, in turn, more valuable.

. . .

High Quality = Quality is a difficult aspect of digital art because art is subjective. What you'll need to do when figuring out the level of quality in an art piece is understand the artist, their work, how it compares, and just a general gut feeling. There's no real right or wrong way of going about determining quality. Some art pieces will immediately answer this question, but some might take more analysis.

Undervalued = Mispricing of NFTs happens all the time. However, what I really mean when I say this has a lot to do with predicting the future or at least making a prediction. So, when you find an NFT that seems undervalued, ask yourself why. If it's because the artist, musician, sports player, game, etc., is new, but you can see that they might be a major name in the future, then jump on the opportunity while you can.

- **What Should You Be Focusing On?**

The best thing to focus on when trying to find and buy NFTs is looking for those unique pieces. Of course, I'm talking about the ones that tick all the boxes I mentioned before. Finding an NFT that checks all three isn't impossible, but it is challenging.

The most important one by far is focusing on undervalued cryptoart. Seeing a low price but realizing that there's so much more to a certain piece than meets the eye is a skill many would kill for, so hopefully, you've got a knack for finding hidden gems.

. . .

Never invest in something just because it's an NFT. Instead, invest because you believe it truly has the potential to appreciate in value.

When To Sell Your NFTs

Buying NFTs always leads to a conundrum down the line. Do I HODL (hold on for dear life) my NFT or do I sell it? When is the right time for even selling an NFT?

- **HODL**

The 'holding on for dear life' approach usually is rooted in a belief that the NFT you managed to snap up has a great deal of potential to become worth far more than what you paid for it. The only other reason why you might HODL an NFT is when you want to keep it, not for investing purposes, but for your own personal collection.

A great example of how HODL can work in your favor is CryptoPunks. Granted, this was an NFT back when NFTs were truly in their infancy, but still. The value of CryptoPunks remained relatively low for years, having started at an average of 0.173 Ether in 2017 to what it's worth today, which is an average of 80 Ether.

- **Trading Regularly**

If you're going into NFTs to trade regularly, then it's unlikely you'll be deterred from that goal. However, it's essential to be careful of letting go of NFTs that are not yet at their fullest potential in terms of value. You never really know 100% where an NFT will go, but there are signs that guide you to understanding if it's worth offloading or HODL instead.

- **The Right Time To Sell**

Selling an NFT is a time-sensitive decision. You want to ensure that you're going to actually get something out of selling it at this moment or what's the point of selling it at all? Unfortunately, many people manage to amass relatively good collections to begin trading with, and then they completely fumble the trading part. That's the problem. Trading NFTs is a two-part process of finding good, quality NFTs and then trading them effectively. While you can be less than amazing at the first part, if you're bad at the second part, you're in trouble.

You need to have an interest in the NFT you're trying to sell before listing it. That interest can be coming from anywhere. It could be for the art itself, or it could be because the artist is now blowing up, and everyone wants to grab their art while they can. Everything should be considered before just going off and relisting your NFT.

- **Additional Costs**

When trying to calculate profit potential, you need to consider some things that will eat away at that profit. For example, fees like gas and listing fees, and royalties are almost always unavoidable. Of course, they differ from marketplace to marketplace, but they do exist for the most part.

You also have to consider price appreciation or depreciation. The market is volatile, and these things change in an instant. So keep up to date with everything so that you're not in the dark or caught off guard.

Alternative NFT Investment: NFT Stock

If you want to invest in NFTs but not by buying NFTs, there are other options. However, the main option I want to focus on is NFT stocks. There are many NFT stock options available as more and more companies have become involved in the NFT market or formed as a result of it.

- **Funko**

Listed on the NASDAQ as FNKO, Funko is a well-known brand for pop-culture consumer products, so it might be really surprising to see them being mentioned as an NFT stock investment opportunity. In April of 2021, the company acquired a significant stake in TokenWave. TokenWave is well known for being the developer of TokenHead, which is a mobile app and a website for showcasing NFT holding while tracking them.

Funko began launching their NFT offerings on WAX recently, which is the leading decentralized wallet the blockchain has to offer. They're continuing to make big moves and solidify their presence in the market.

- **Mattel**

Giant toy-maker Mattel, famous for its brand Hot Wheels, launched the Hot Wheel NFT Garage series in June of 2021. They were very successful, and considering Mattel's extensive product portfolio, including the likes of Barbie, UNO, American

Girl, and so on, many see a great deal of potential for the brand and NFTs.

- **Cloudflare**

The cloud computing company has been focused for years on providing security and business solution tools for consumers. Now they're doing all of that while supporting and curating NFTs. In April of 2021, they announced that Cloudflare Stream would support NFTs and allowed creators and developers to embed NFTs into their videos.

- **Coinbase**

Coinbase has been around for some time, having established itself in 2012. Operating in over 100 countries, Coinbase is an easy-to-use crypto exchange platform where fiat money can be converted into cryptocurrency. Now they've added an NFT marketplace so people can also trade NFTs.

- **CleanSpark**

CleanSpark is a mining company that focuses on sustainable crypto. They use more energy-efficient methods like microgrids, renewables, and other means to keep the emission low or non-existent that's what CleanSpart is all about. In addition, they are consistently adding in new machines with a goal of 3.2 exahash of computing power come the end of 2022.

- **Why Entertain NFT Investments**

Most people who engage more with NFT investments than actual NFTs do so for excellent reasons.

1. They want to be in on NFTs but aren't keen on the market or fear they don't have the eye for the right assets.
2. Many view it as a safer, less risky investment.
3. Companies that engage in NFTs are involved in multiple revenue streams, diversifying an investment.

Key Takeaway

Many people are under the impression that getting into NFTs is difficult. Still, you'd be surprised how easy it is to start investing. Although the use of cryptocurrencies and exploring the NFT marketplaces can be intimidating and risky, it's worth the risks. Investing in NFTs, building a collection, or creating NFTs of your own are risky investments that can pay off handsomely.

It's essential to always compare the world of NFTs to stocks. Both NFTs and the stock market can make people a lot of money, but they can also lose a person a lot of money. When investing, it's crucial to keep this in mind because you should never over-extend yourself. Don't put in money you cannot afford to lose! Otherwise, take those risks and make wise decisions. You never know how they might pay off.

5

MORE THAN INVESTING

INVESTING in NFTs is the leading way most people make money in this space, but there's more that can be done to earn some serious money in the crypto space. Although I've already told you about the NFT creators making millions of dollars selling their cryptoart, what's to say you can't be the next TechnoPicasso? That's right, nothing! While Beeple made an eye-watering $69 million, that's not going to be the case for everyone. So I want to be realistic with you. While you can definitely make serious money, don't aim for the sun just yet.

In this chapter, I will tell you how you can make money from NFTs in other ways beyond investing. From creating and renting out NFTs, there are many exciting ways to make money work for you, thanks to cryptoart. So while you might not end up being $69 million richer, you can definitely still wind up being richer at the end of the day.

Some Of The Creators Making Waves

Since 2019, we've been hearing stories of early artists who came to the table and considered NFTs and ran with it and are now reaping the benefits of their decision. Artists like Sarah Zucker, Tesla and SpaceX's Elon Musk, NFL player Rob Gronkowski, even musicians like Shawn Mendez are all minting and selling NFTs.

Some are having insane success, but for the most part, these bigger names are making a fair amount of money from their blockchain endeavors. Sarah Zucker, for example, started selling in 2019. By 2021 she'd made over $274,000. This is happening to a lot of people. More prominent celebrities might make in the millions, which is excellent for them. It's hard not to ignore the incredible achievements artists like Sarah Zucker are making.

Smaller, less well-known artists are staking their claim on the blockchain. They're taking control of their own careers and making a great living off doing so. It should be a source of inspiration to see artists finally breaking free of the 'starving artist' moniker they've had over them for so long.

Another great example is the Chicago-based artist Kane. The 40-year-old artist was painting oil paintings which he's been selling for years. He learned how to code and eventually made software which he used to create his art, and he too began selling NFTs in 2019. By late 2020, Kane was a record holder for a while, having sold a piece titled 'Right Place & Right Time' for over $100,000. He's now making over that figure annually. It's a true testament to the empowerment artists are getting from their work being appreciated on the blockchain. This is a powerful testament to the power of NFTs for artists of all calibers.

Creating Your Own NFTs

Getting into the NFTs with the hope of making money isn't easy. First, it requires the creation and marketing of your own NFTs. Creating cryptoart has proven to be the most tried and true method of making money on the blockchain from NFTs. The process of doing so, well, it's filled with a ton of steps that we're about to explore.

- **Deciding What You're Creating**

First things first, you need to consider what you're actually making. As mentioned in previous chapters, NFTs aren't just one specific thing. You've got a lot of options handy to make something creative, from cryptoart to music and beyond. But cryptoart is where the money is, which is why it should be your primary focus.

But this is really the easiest part of the process. So many other decisions need to be made before you even come close to creating your NFT.

- **Keys To Making Money From Your NFTs**

There are a few tips I can share with you that are important to remember when trying to make your digital assets more appealing and worth the price tag. They require a focus on:

- Scarcity
- Discoverability
- Promotion
- Resales & Royalties

- **Scarcity**

I think many people assume the best course of action going into NFTs is to create in abundance. This is probably the biggest mistake I've seen new NFT artists make. The problem when you're in the business of mass-producing NFTs is that the transparency of your intentions really takes over, and people aren't looking to invest in grifts and the grifters attached to them.

A genuine quality over quantity approach will give you a much better leg up than if you were to throw everything at the wall hoping something resonates. There's a way to do this effectively. For example, you can engage in limited runs and set hard supply limits for each month. Another option is creating artificial rarity, which means you take your NFTs and use pricing variations, making some NFTs more expensive or inexpensive than the others. Using the artificial rarity approach means defining the scarcity, so investors know what they're getting.

- **Discoverability**

As you learned in Chapter 4, there are a ton of marketplaces. Like with scarcity, new NFT artists assume the approach is to get on as many as possible. Incorrect. You want to focus on one or two platforms, usually the ones that most align with your vision and goals. Working with one or two platforms means you're focusing on bettering your existence on those algorithms and not spreading yourself too thin. Discoverability comes from algorithms, and you need to cultivate a presence and establish consistency to make an impression on these algorithms to prove you're worth paying attention to in the long run.

The other means of establishing discoverability is by linking your NFT seller profile on social media and other outlets that can direct traffic to your digital store.

- **Promotion**

If nobody knows about your NFT, nobody buys your NFT. So it really doesn't matter how great it is if nobody knows about it. Promotion can be just about anything:

- Social media marketing
- Paid advertising
- Mentions on influencer pages
- Mentions on influential crypto/blockchain/NFT sites

This extends to anything else that might generate interest in your NFTs.

- **Resales & Royalties**

In the past, art was commissioned, and once that obligation was met, the artist signed over all rights to their work forever. However, NFTs are redefining the monetization of artwork in the most radical and equitable ways. By selling NFTs, artists are not only entitled to the initial royalty but also royalties on every transaction that artwork undergoes for the rest of its existence.

. . .

This also means that artists can focus not just on making money on the initial sale but also on how their work can exist and benefit them long-term.

Royalty schemes are opt-ins on most platforms. They allow for customization with the amount of kickback, which is usually up to 10%, and then they pay it out once a month. This has really changed the balance of power for artists and redefined what ownership of creative work really means.

How To Create Your Own NFTs

Now it's time to get to the actual task: creating the NFTs. This process is drawn out initially because it requires certain decisions that will define your NFT career for a while. These decisions cover things like which blockchain, market, and wallet you'll use, among other necessary decisions and considerations.

So let's get into the process of creating your own NFT.

- **Deciding on a Blockchain**

The first step you will need to decide on is which blockchain you will be hosting your NFTs on. Every blockchain has its own way of doing things; no blockchain operates the same way. As a result, you need to decide which best suits your needs.

Ethereum remains the most popular and the most powerful, but it's not the only one. Many blockchain options are available, like Polkadot, Cosmos, Free TON, among others. However, for argument's sake, I will focus on Ethereum to explain how you'll go about setting up and selling your NFTs. This process is more often than not adaptable to other blockchains, albeit with subtle differences.

- **Creating a Wallet**

We already know a lot about wallets, thanks to Chapter 4. So you might have already successfully created an Ethereum wallet. When choosing which wallet you're going to go with, you've determined if it's a hot or cold wallet.

Hot wallets remain connected to the internet, while cold wallets aren't connected 24/7. Cold wallets are only connected to the internet during transactions, which is when they become 'hot.' When they're cold, they remain hidden and undetectable. Hence, they're far less susceptible to hacks from cybercriminals.

If you're new to crypto, it's probably best to stick to a hot wallet while continuing to explore what a cold wallet is and how to operate one. Hot wallets are also free, which is beneficial for newbies without the initial capital when starting out in NFTs.

- **Deciding on a Marketplace**

In chapter 4, we discussed NFT marketplaces in-depth. The most popular options are:

- OpenSea
- Mintable
- Nifty

- Gateway
- Rarible
- Mintbase

Once you've weighed your options and determined which platform suits your needs as an artist best, you need to connect your wallet to the platform you've decided on.

- **Minting Your NFT**

Now that you've gotten a lot of the leg work done, it's time to mint your very first NFT. You're going to click on the minting option, create that new item, and now it's time for yet another decision. Are you going gasless or traditional? Also, what does that even mean?

When a transaction is gasless, it's free however it won't show up in your wallet until a sale takes place. In the meantime they exist on Ethereum in secret, lurking in the shadows, patiently waiting. When you go traditional it's there and ready to go immediately. It also comes at a price. That price is paying the transaction fee upfront which is 2.5%. When it comes to transaction fees which can cost roughly $99, gasless transactions are usually charged at 5%. If you're a professional artist, you should go with the traditional option. If you're new and trying everything out, go gasless for your first time and advance when you're comfortable.

- **Listing Your NFT**

When you're listing your NFT you'll be provided with some options for how you'd like to sell the NFT. Those options are rather straightforward:

- **Fixed Price** - meaning that the price it's listed at is the price that must be paid to get the NFT.
- **Auction** - people can bid and others can challenge and outbid until one comes out victorious.
- **Auction with Buy Now option** - essentially a hybrid where people can bid, but there's a nuclear option for the person looking to take gold and buy it outright at usually a higher fee than what the bids might end up being. It's a risky move for a newbie to engage in this option.

Once you've listed your NFT, your next step is to go and market that NFT to death, or at least until it's sold.

- **Creating Your NFT for Free**

There are ways to create and list an NFT for free. There are so many instances where this is possible, but let's look at OpenSea and the Polygon (MATIC) blockchain. The way you avoid paying anything is by evading the gas fee. The process of creating an NFT for free on the Polygon blockchain using OpenSea is similar to any other system. It's such a straightforward process that really only needs to be boiled down to one change which is selecting the right blockchain.

Minting an NFT is far easier than actually selling one, so get ready for the real challenge which is marketing your NFT.

Marketing & Selling Your NFTs,

I've said it before, and I'll say it again, market your NFTs! People need to know you and your work exist, and that only comes from creating a solid presence online. Not just on the blockchain all over the online world.

Here are some ways you can increase the visibility and hype of your NFTs.

- **Advertising Your NFTs**

There are many great options available for you to promote your NFTs to the right audience. You're looking to find the people interested in the market and who could potentially buy your NFT. Here are some of the ways you can entice and lure them onto your seller's page so they can see your collections.

- **NFT Calendar**

Think of this as the index of NFTs where new NFT drops are collected across the numerous marketplaces and mentioned all in one place. This is where NFT collectors search for NFTs easier as they don't have to go across all the platforms.

To add your NFT to this calendar, you need to follow a few simple steps, which mainly revolve around the details of the NFT or NFT drop:

1. NFT title
2. About you (the creator)
3. Description of the piece

4. Key visuals
5. Time and date of the drop
6. The marketplace where the drops are available
7. Link to the release

Once this release date is submitted, it's reviewed and uploaded to the calendar for all to see.

- **Social Media**

Social media is a great way to get in touch with your target audience. First, however, you must focus on the social media platforms where your target audience congregates online. For example, you can't expect Facebook to yield great sales when the majority of active users on Facebook are out of the age range you're looking to sell to.

The social media avenues you want to focus on include Reddit, Discord, Clubhouse, and Twitter. Reddit has a ton of NFT, crypto, and blockchain boards where you can chat with like-minded people and, in some cases, promote your work. Discord allows you to join channels where people constantly communicate about the NFT world and all its developments. You could even start your own community and grow that, providing yourself and other artists a space to market their work to potential customers. Clubhouse is an audio-based platform where you communicate by talking to your audience. You can find exciting ways of promoting your work this way, maybe by promoting yourself and your journey as the brand and the products as a byproduct of that brand. Finally, the most important is Twitter. You might think that sounds crazy, but

Twitter is great for NFT lovers, both sellers, and buyers alike. They stay up to date on the blockchain world while promoting their work and sharing art and products they love.

These aren't the only social media platforms. Of course, there's also Instagram, Snapchat, etc. But these are the prominent ones in this particular space.

- **Word of Mouth**

Get the word out there and make those you spread the word to initially spread the word further. This is most effective with other artists, especially ones you've developed a relationship with where maybe they've asked you to do the same. It's not an IOU situation; it's friends supporting friends. Be sure not to expect anybody to do, and don't berate them if they don't, instead focus on getting as many people as possible to share your work and drive them to the website.

- **Featured Drops & Marketplaces Newsletters**

These are two options that involve direct communication with marketplaces. It's worth talking to these platforms and figuring out how you can get on their featured pages and their marketplace newsletters. Some marketplaces change these weekly, advertising roughly 4-5 upcoming drops, and some even make it to their socials. The same goes for newsletters. These marketplace newsletters are sent out weekly detailing some of the exciting drops coming to their platform in the coming weeks or days. You might get rejected, but you don't know until you try, and if you are rejected, keep trying with each new drop until they give you the coveted spot.

- **Influencers**

Influencers are down to sell anything. You can find ones with the right amount of impressions and audience size to make a real difference very easily with platforms that help you find influencers. Sometimes it is not about the sales but the increased traffic. As more people start visiting and interacting on your store, the platforms recognize and reward the traffic increases thinking you're extremely popular and a great fit for homepage territory. But sure, making sales is also great. Influencers can promote anything from you as an artist to a single NFT or a whole drop!

- **PR Agency**

PR Agencies can be very useful in getting the word out there about your NFTs. They've got insider knowledge; they know who to speak to and how to speak to them. It's the best third-party method of getting into newspapers, magazines, websites, etc. But, of course, you can also do this yourself by reaching out to newspapers, having a website, posting blogs announcing drops, or building an audience on Medium, Substack, and other news and newsletter services.

- **Tips for Advertising & Promoting**

Here are some quick tips for getting you started:

1. Get your own website where you can promote your work without any barriers to entry.
2. Initiate collaborations with reputable brands, influencers, musicians, artists, and whoever is willing to give you the time of day.
3. Organize some giveaways to hype up your collection or

to help build a reputation that benefits you for future drops and collaborations.

4. Don't wait till the last minute to promote your drop. Start planning well in advance and initiating contact well before you release.
5. Create a 'white list' so people have exclusive access to your NFTs before things get crazy and everyone is after it. This creates a sense of priority and exclusivity that sometimes drives up the value of the NFT.

- **Pricing Your NFT**

The mere thought of pricing can send some creators into full-blown panic mode as they try to figure out what is right and wrong in terms of their price. So here are some guidelines to help you determine the price of your NFT.

- **Starting Out**

There are three levels of pricing to consider; wide range, mid-range, and luxury/premium range. This is the average price of each range:

- **Wide Range:** .02 ETH

- **Mid-Range:** .06 ETH

- **Luxury/Premium Range:** 1 ETH

The wide range pricing model makes it low enough that it's accessible to the widest possible audience. At the same time, it's still higher than gas and transaction fees therefore you'll still make some money with larger returns being seen over time from royalties as your reputation and demand for your work hopefully grows.

- **Established Artist**

When you're a more established artist, you've got the power to set your prices somewhat higher than the entry-level seller might be able to set them at. Now don't let this get to your head. It's important to remember that overcharging will not result in sales, even if you're established.

- **Wide Range:** 1 ETH

- **Mid-Range:** 2 ETH

- **Luxury/Premium Range:** 3 ETH

- **What Makes For Higher Prices?**

There are some elements of an NFT that can increase its value and, therefore, its price. For example, adding unlockables can incentivize buyers and collectors to purchase your NFT. Things like allowing limited physical copies of the artwork to hang on their walls, adding in physical items to almost sweeten the deal, or even providing a discount code for future NFT purchases.

The best indicator that you're in a position to start raising your prices is when something you create gets into a bidding war. This is a clear identifier that your reputation is gaining strength, and your work is more valuable.

- **Tips for Pricing Your NFTs**

When it comes to pricing, there are some things you should know to help demystify the process so you're never caught off guard. Of course, you want to go in with crystal clear goals, all while remaining firmly in reality.

- It's important to always aim for the sun while starting on the ground. You want to build your way up and build a reputation worthy of higher fees. When you aim high and start there too, you'll find you get nowhere. So start out with a sense of humility and steadily raise the bar.
- Don't ever allow yourself to confine your work to a set standard. Artists experiment, and you're an artist, aren't you? So experiment. Do things that seem wild and wacky. Art is limitless unless you make it otherwise.
- Avoid thinking of Ether as fiat money. You don't want to let a mischaracterization of Ether be the catalyst for the overvaluation of your art. But, on the other hand, you've also got to acknowledge your position when you start pricing your work. It's not a decision based on what you believe you should be getting. It's about what is possible.
- Don't be married to one platform. Experiment with other platforms and figure out which ones work best for you and your work. If you start on OpenSea but hate it, why would you stay there? It makes no sense. Never commit outright to one platform. Shop around. It's essential, however, to ensure your pricing is consistent across the board. Don't overcharge on one and undercharge on another; users are keenly aware of what's happening in the space, and they talk. You don't want to be the subject of ranting posts on subreddits and Discord channels.
- Always be aware of upcoming updates and how they affect you, your NFTs, and their pricing.

- Always pay attention to the secondary market and opportunities that exist in this space, from royalties to NFT fragments and beyond.

Other ways to earn from NFTs

There are many unique ways to make money from NFTs that exist beyond the traditional means of selling and royalties from resales. Before I break them all down, it's essential to understand that some of these opportunities are very new. There are risks involved, just like there are risks involved all across the world of NFTs and the blockchain. Okay, let's get into some exciting ways you can earn money from NFTs beyond traditional means.

- **Fractional NFTs**

Fractional NFTs is pretty much exactly how it sounds; it's an NFT divided into fractions. As the NFT owner, you split the NFT into pieces in the form of ERC-20 tokens. These can be used on decentralized finance applications and, therefore, allow more people to own part of an NFT, which brings liquidity to the market.

- **Renting Out NFTs**

It might sound bizarre to know that renting out an NFT is possible, but considering what you now know about the blockchain, is it? Renting out an NFT is an excellent method of making a passive income. It's even better when the NFT is in demand.

The best instance of renting out NFTs is digital trading cards; think of the game Axie as an example. Players love having new cards to use to increase their odds. Renting out NFTs makes use of smart contracts where you are free to set the terms of how long and how much the rental agreement will be.

The best platform for this type of passive income stream is reNFT. The current daily rates on reNFT usually range on average from 0.002 to 2 wrapped Ethereum (WETH).

Wrapped Ethereum is the ERC-20 version of ether, Ethereum's native cryptocurrency.

- **Stake NFTs**

A major benefit of NFTs and decentralized financing protocols is the new possibilities in terms of staking NFTs. What does this mean? Well, staking NFTs refers to a process of depositing digital assets into decentralized finance protocol smart contracts in order to generate a yield.

There are a lot of platforms that support a wide variety of NFTs, such as Kira Networks, NFTX, Splinterlands, and Only1. While other platforms might require users to purchase native NFTs, which allows you to earn staking token rewards.

There are some cases where the rewards that are distributed to 'stakers' are denominated in governance tokens. This gives token holders voting rights for the future developments of their ecosystem. Beyond this, however, it's possible to reinvest the coins earned into yield generating protocols.

- **Liquidity to Earn**

As decentralized finance becomes more intertwined with NFTs, the possibilities become more significant than ever before. One of these opportunities is providing liquidity and getting NFTs in return to establish your standing in an existing liquidity pool.

By providing liquidity, an automated market maker (AMM) issues an ERC-721 token, aka an LP-NFT, that details your share of the total amount locked in the pool. These NFTs are also loaded with the token pair you deposited, symbols, and the pool's address. You're then able to sell this NFT to quickly liquidate your positions on liquidity pools.

- **Farm for Yields**

Yield farming is an interesting concept. It's partly possible because automated market makers utilize and rely more and more on NFTs, which makes farming yields with NFT-powered products more possible. This method works by leveraging various decentralized financing protocols to generate the highest possible yield with your already owned digital assets.

Key Takeaway

The key takeaway here should be that if you're an artist or a creator in any creative medium, there's space for you in NFTs. You have the opportunity to take control of your own career by creating NFTs, marketing them and yourself in the process, and making money for the rest of your arts lifetime. There's even a chance you increase your income exponentially in the process. You never really know what's going to happen when it comes to NFTs and your participation in this new digital system.

. . .

It's more important than ever to get into the game considering how many others are doing just that as we speak. You need to find new and exciting ways to stand out. If you want to sell your art, which I'm sure you do, then you need to put in the effort. Not just into the artwork itself, which is essential, but also the marketing of your art and you as an artist.

6

GETTING INTO THE FINE PRINT

CryptoArt has been steadily gaining ground as a pillar of NFTs and the power of the blockchain for a few years now. However, in 2021 instead of gaining ground, it began skyrocketing. While cryptoart is a relatively new form of investment and technology, there's no underscoring its newfound value in an increasingly digital world.

While this popularity is thriving and continuing to grow with every NFT sale, there's no denying that there's still a lot we've failed to understand about NFTs, which extends to the law and taxation. Due to the blockchain being this completely unregulated digital landscape, we soon realize that many aspects of this new technology can be vague and somewhat unclear. In some cases, we find ourselves operating from a gray area where things aren't as black and white as we'd perhaps prefer.

. . .

In this chapter, we're going to explore the fine print of NFTs, crypto, and the blockchain so you can confidently navigate this legal minefield.

Intellectual Property Rights

So here's the unfortunate news. Just because you own an NFT doesn't mean you own the copyright. There are virtually no intellectual property rights when it comes to NFTs. This is because NFTs are developed displaying an underlying artwork. Therefore, the artist or owner doesn't hold underlying intellectual property rights.

The copyright and all other intellectual property rights usually remain with the creator of the artwork or digital asset. Buyers of NFTs are then given a right to display the underlying asset. Creators use intellectual property rights to protect their work even when they no longer own it outright. Considering they're continuously getting royalties from each sale, it makes it more in line with how the blockchain works. It's a real power to the artist type of movement.

Artists have the ability to set the terms of the deal. For example, they can set up recurring royalty payments, one-time payments, commission on resale, etc. When a buyer breaches these terms and conditions, it can even result in their accounts being terminated on certain marketplaces.

At the end of it all, the original owner of the NFT is the one with all the power and is the copyright holder. Anyone who buys the NFT just gets to use the copyrighted art in relation to the token's individual usage capabilities. If there's a disagreement on either side of breaches in the intellectual property rights, it usually heads to litigation.

What's often lost on buyers of NFTs is how much power the original owner actually has over the digital asset they're selling. The artist/owner usually retains the rights to copy, distribute, modify, publicly perform, and publicly display the artwork any which way they please unless explicitly granted to someone else. When you're unaware of these powers the copyright holder has, you risk doing something that in turn infringes on the copyright, and that opens you up to litigation. It's important to be very careful when navigating around the minefield that is copyright laws, and this applies to anything creative.

Data Protection Laws

There are existing data protection laws that allow users to obliterate their personal data. However, if you've been paying attention, you'll remember that the blockchain isn't really about that way of life. The blockchain is unchangeable. What happens on the blockchain stays on the blockchain forever.

Another aspect of data protection laws is that they allow users to change and rectify inaccurate personal data. Unfortunately, the blockchain in its current form makes exercising this right nearly impossible. This means that, in theory, NFTs which contain your personal information forever are potentially violating these long-standing data protection laws.

. . .

Most people go into NFT understanding this is a reality of the blockchain. They accept the terms and conditions that have existed since the development and founding of the blockchain. However, many people who engage with the blockchain near-daily remain somewhat unaware of these laws and NFTs breaching of these laws in the first place.

Data Hosting & Storage

In terms of storage, NFTs and the digital asset they're representing are usually stored separately. The NFT exists on the blockchain and is connected to the digital asset via a link. The NFT on the blockchain contains the data and transaction history but doesn't have the actual digital asset present.

The problem with this lies in the fact that because the digital asset doesn't exist on the blockchain if it were to be deleted or heaven forbid the service hosting the digital asset fails, goes offline, or anything else that might disrupt the hosting of the digital asset it breaks the link between NFT and asset.

As a result, the NFT exists without an asset attached, and it's rendered nearly worthless. Remember, there's a word I've used a lot of times to describe an NFT, and it should explain why this is such an issue without an option to fix it. NFTs are unique. They simply cannot be replaced. What's worse, if you're the unlucky owner of that NFT that's now got a broken NFT, there are no true recourse options. The blockchain largely remains a lawless land.

While regular laws might apply, such as regulatory record-keeping violations, it's hard to really apply laws designated for a completely separate entity to the blockchain. Considering it's all people really have to use to make a case they're trying. Beyond violations of the law, this presents a clear potential danger for loss of data and business interruptions that remain far beyond the owner of the NFT. There's no such scenario where any guarantees are made that nothing will happen because you truly never know what might happen. This is one of the factors that add to NFTs' riskiness.

Payment of Royalties

Royalties on NFTs are achieved through the use of a smart contract which is composed in NFTs code. This contract makes distributing money to the original creator possible. As the seller gets their money, some of the money is sent to the original owner immediately upon selling that cryptoart piece.

In order to achieve this system, the NFT has to be resold on the same platform. It can't migrate elsewhere to another marketplace. Unfortunately, American laws are far behind on NFTs and crypto at large, so there are no laws that distinguish resale rights. As a result of this, there's no recourse in the event of unpaid royalties.

At the end of the day, this results in that if a seller buys an NFT of marketplace A but then eventually sells it on marketplace B, the creator isn't compensated or paid royalties. There's nothing stopping them from taking it to another marketplace, and it's possible they're completely unaware of what happens when they do take it elsewhere. So understand that when you make a decision like this, for whatever reason, it's affecting someone else negatively.

. . .

This problem isn't a uniquely American one, but in comparison to the European Union, Great Britain, roughly 70 other jurisdictions, the laws are not there to provide the artists with proper protections.

Estate & Sequence Planning

When someone dies, they leave behind their worldly possessions and assets to pass along to their heirs. As a result, the legal frameworks that handle digital collectibles upon the death of the owner are relatively similar everywhere. That doesn't mean you shouldn't check local law, but rest assured that it's likely very similar, if not slightly different in wording.

When planning a personal Estate plan, you've got to be strategic in including NFTs into your plans. Why does it require strategic planning? Well, NFTs are extremely secure and can only be accessed via a personal key and a password. Now you likely don't want to be keeping written records of these passwords and security keys for obvious reasons, so what do you do?

The most common recommendation is assigning a representative that has access to your digital wallet should anything happen to you. They'll be able to administer them in the event of your death. You want to ensure that the person in charge is trustworthy, as they'll have access to your account, which in the wrong hands can be devastating for your 'digital legacy.' Giving out your password and security keys always has a risk associated with it, cyber-hacking, theft, etc. There are ways of avoiding giving out your information and only releasing it in the most necessary circumstances. For example, you could use a third-party system where backup keys via special multi-sig wallets are issued. This gives trustees power to withdraw funds and do what the owner initially wanted in accordance with the final will.

One of the most common methods used to pass on digital assets is through trusts. This works by storing your password and security key in a digital legacy where trustees are given control over your assets upon death, both digital and physical. In an increasingly online world, it's important that if you were to ever go down this path to find trustees that actually understand the market. This means understanding their volatility, as well as their diversification powers. Shop around before just jumping on the first trust you find. Once you've decided, it's time to get the attorneys involved and draft a powers and responsibilities document together with the trustees.

In the event that an NFT hasn't been included in an estate plan or trust, the assets might just be eliminated entirely. This is why ensuring that you've got the information stored securely in an accessible form for someone to review upon your death is essential. Nobody wants your hard work to be lost to the blockchain forever. Once it's gone, it's gone. There is no getting it back, and it's important to understand that reality. Not planning ahead means your digital legacy being reduced to a tragic tale of password mismanagement.

Right of Publicity

Right of Publicity is a rather common law that prevents commercial exploitation of individuals, regardless of the person, likeness, and overall identity, without the individual's consent.

So how does this affect NFT creators? Well, some creators have gone and taken the likes of celebrities and created NFTs with their likeness and sold them on the blockchain as minted NFTs. This has become the basis of legal questions about how and if it breaks the law. Even outside of NFTs, this is a question that is raised all the time as people create and sell things that feature celebrities, influential people, and sometimes just some random person we've never heard of until a case grabs national headlines.

Judges approach the law differently regardless of where you are. Their verdict is influenced by their understanding of the complaint, in this case, NFTs. The problem is that NFTs aren't widely known or understood. This has resulted in ill-equipped judges handling cases that they understand but not enough to make a truly informed decision.

Laws just haven't caught up to NFTs enough yet to make the rules surrounding this crystal clear. Right now, judges are interpreting the law based on new technology and a law that was written before that technology existed. So sometimes, the rulings don't align with that law.

When the law is upheld, the creators of the NFTs can be in for some unfortunate penalties that can range from compensatory and punitive damages or statutory damages, and finally all the way to equitable relief in the form of disgorgement of profits.

Not gaining consent to use someone's likeness might make you a quick sale now, and maybe provide you with a healthy cash influx, but they can come at a costly price down the line. From damages to legal fees, you might spend far more than the NFT ever made in the first place.

So what do you do? It's simple, avoid using people's likeness without consent. You never know if you're going to get litigated to death over a right of publicity dispute, but the chance is one that comes at a heavy price. Creators should be crafting strategies to avoid using the likeness of others altogether.

Creators need to also remember that the right to publicity can extend to characters in entertainment. A case in California where an artist created a depiction of The Three Stooges was challenged in court. The judge scrutinized the defense's argument that the depiction was protected under the first amendment but did state that if the works had been sufficiently altered or transformed from the original, it might be protected under the first amendment. This is a clear-cut example of people navigating and writing the laws in real-time by using precedent as a compass. The only downside about this can be if you're the one who's precedent-setting in the worst-case scenario.

Taking risks and chances in the world of NFTs is great, but understand the potential costs attached to those risks. Make sure you're ready and willing to defend your risks and if you're not, create a strategy to work around any instances of the right of publicity violations.

Regulatory Implications

Understand that the laws thus far have not caught up with NFTs, cryptocurrency, or the blockchain. Now that it's becoming clear just how entrenched it's going to be in our lives as the decade presses on, lawmakers are racing to establish regulations.

When new and innovative things come along, they usually don't get categorized with everything else. Instead, they get their own set of laws. Right now, the focus is on securities, anti-money laundering, and customer procedures.

- **Security Law Compliance**

As it stands, NFT marketplaces are fractionalizing NFTs to allow for numerous traders to take part in expensive proposals. This is leading to varying characterizations, but one that's coming up the most is characterizing NFTs as a result of this practice in the same way one might describe an index fund.

What this means is that NFTs are acting like stocks traded as fractionalized tokens on certain marketplaces. This has led members of the SEC to label these as unregistered securities. This isn't a widely supported assessment, but if it were to gather support and result in regulatory action, it means the NFT investments people have made are at risk.

- **Anti-Money Laundering Mechanisms**

The world of NFTs is largely unregulated and uncharted waters for regulators. They're grappling with the realities that there's a lot that is possible with NFTs, both positive and negative, legal and illegal and that they need to respond by regulating. That's something everyone can agree on. It's the actual regulations that are causing these types of regulating efforts to languish indefinitely.

The Anti-Money Laundering (AML) regulating bodies are noticing how the SEC is dealing with securities and is paying close attention to efforts of their own to regulate. AML laws in the United States have extended to apply to certain cases and dealers where these regulations might head; however, it is a question that has no concrete answer.

The US government has been expanding some of its AML provisions in the National Defense Authorization Act (NDAA) which provided updates to existing laws such as the Bank Secrecy Act (BSA), the Corporate Transparency Act (CTA), and the Anti-Money Laundering Act (AMLA). The ultimate determination has been that NFTs are not equal to antiquities. This has given them more power to have traders reach more AML requirements to ensure the transactions are legit and genuinely transparent.

- **Know Your Customer Procedures**

Know Your Customers is a process in which a user's identity has to be regularly verified both in the initial stages of account creation and periodically over time. Lawmakers are trying to find ways to protect users' data. The hope is that by treating these emerging technologies in line with financial institutions, they might be able to change enough to make it truly a viable option. The other side of this is that over-regulation can lead to vulnerabilities, stagnation, or decline of emerging technologies until they're rendered obsolete. We're far from knowing which side of the coin this issue lands on.

NFTs & The Courts

We've yet to see excessive NFT cases popping up in courts around the world, or even just across the fifty states, but in 2021, the first-ever NFT lawsuit was filed. That lawsuit was filed between Jeeun Friel, the plaintiff, and Dapper Labs Inc and the CEO of Dapper Labs in the case of Jeeun Friel vs. Dapper Labs and Roham Gharegozlou. The lawsuit alleged that Dapper Labs' platform, formally known as NBA Top Shot, had sold securities when it sold NFTs on its platform. It was alleged this was a clear violation of securities laws.

Once the judgment has been made on Jeeun Friel's lawsuit, it could serve as a landmark case for the world of NFTs. This might answer the question; should NFTs be treated as 'securities' or not.

Another good example of a high-profile legal case on NFTs is the legal battle between Roc-A-Fella Records and Jay-Z's former business partner Damon Dash. The courts sided with Jay-Z after Dash attempted to sell Jay-Z's album 'Reasonable Doubt' as an NFT. They found the attempt to sell virtual ownership of the album's copyright to be an act of conversion and unjust enrichment.

The more cases that wind up in court facing judgment, the more the laws are written in the eyes of the judges simply based on precedent. It's important to note that precedent doesn't always mean it will go the way you think. Every judge thinks differently, but these precedents are acknowledged, respected, and used to form opinions and consensus on legal matters where the laws are easily misinterpreted or not clearly defined. NFTs currently operate on laws that were written before they existed. There's a reliance on old creative laws and various other laws to self-regulate the industry in the eyes of the laws. If lawmakers come to the table and decide on these laws, this can change, but that seems far off right now.

Taxes

Ah yes, the dreaded word everybody hates no matter what: taxes. You knew it was coming, and here we are, diving headfirst into a world of financial pain.

Before we continue, I feel I should provide a disclaimer. Everything I'm about to mention primarily relates to the United States. Therefore, it's essential to understand your country's laws surrounding NFTs. The laws in your country can be vastly different from the United States approach. Arguably, the US is a government that hasn't made much progress in understanding and regulating NFTs, or crypto for that matter.

- **Taxable NFT Activities**

The following NFT activities can result in capital gains taxes.

- **Selling**

When you create an NFT, you're not yet executing a taxable event. However, when you list and sell said NFT on a marketplace, then you're in the taxable zone where you'll need to pay taxes on the profit you make. These profits are considered an income and are taxed at the income tax rate. This obviously varies but can range between 10% - 37%. Then there's the self-employment tax of 15.3%.

Any NFT sale performed by owners of the NFT, but not the original artist, either incurs a loss or a profit. Whichever way it goes, you're also incurring a capital gain or capital loss. For example, you purchased an NFT for $5,000 of Ether. You then sold said that NFT for $10,000. That's a capital gain of $5,000, which is taxable.

- **Purchasing**

When you purchase an NFT using cryptocurrencies, the transaction constitutes the disposal of said cryptocurrency. This incurs a capital gain or loss. For example, you purchase an NFT on OpenSea with Ethereum, that's appreciated; well, congratulations, that's a capital gain. However, it is dependent on how long you held on to the Ethereum before it appreciated (or depreciated) in value. The result will make the amount you have to pay different as there's both a long-term capital gains tax and a short-term capital gains tax.

When it's depreciated Etherium, you end up with a capital gains loss, and you can use that to offset other capital gains. So it's a game of checks and balances to lower your overall tax liability.

- **Trading**

When you trade an NFT for another NFT, this triggers a taxable event. For example, you bought an NFT for $3,000 of Ether and then traded it for an NFT worth $4,500 Ether. As a result of this influx of increased worth, you'll incur a taxable capital gain on that $1,500.

- **How You Will Be Taxed as a Creator**

When you create an NFT, you're not yet executing a taxable event. However, when you list and sell said NFT on a marketplace, then you're in the taxable zone where you'll need to pay taxes on the profit you make. These profits are considered an income and are taxed at the income tax rate. This obviously varies but can range between 10% - 37%. Then there's the self-employment tax of 15.3%.

- **NFTs Could Be Taxed as...**

As it stands, the IRS hasn't really made it clear what their policy is on taxing NFTs. This is just a pure example of the dysfunctional world of government where a lack of guidance leads agencies to have to work with outdated measures in order to regulate where they can. It leads to a more haphazard and disconnected approach.

But it goes deeper than that.

- **Property**

The bad news for traders and investors is that NFTs are taxable regardless of your efforts, or lack thereof, to sell the NFT. This is because the current IRS classification for NFT and cryptocurrencies is property. That's right, the word currency lies in the word cryptocurrencies, but that's not how they're taxed.

What this means is that you're going to be technically purchasing and holding onto assets for short periods of time. Considering a vast majority of NFT purchases require cryptocurrencies, you end up buying crypto and spending it in a relatively short space of time. In addition, the value of these cryptocurrencies fluctuates by the hour. These combining factors have led the IRS to view NFTs as a harmless yet taxable 'bate and switch' with the simultaneous purchase of crypto and purchase of assets such as NFT and, in turn, a capital gain or loss. This is why they instead operate on a capital gains system to determine the worth of the profit or loss to decide on how much you're going to pay in taxes. Short-term capital gains work the same as income tax, so it's rather easy to work out.

The IRS uses a method of determining if capital gains is short or long term. When any profits made are held for a year or less, it's considered short-term capital gains. Anything longer than that falls into the long-term capital gains bracket. These different determinations can slightly alter how much you'll end up paying. The amount for long-term capital gains usually ranges between 0% and 20%.

- **Collectibles**

Another method of taxation for NFTs is using a collectibles tax which is akin to what's used for things like stamps, antiques, and other rare collectible items. This tax rate is considerably higher at about 28%. This is only really considered when the assets have been held for longer than a year.

- **Important Things To Remember**

Here are a few more things to remember about taxes and NFTs!

- **Gas fees should be counted in your capital gains.**

When you purchase an NFT, there is usually a gas fee included in the purchase price or expressed as an additional fee unless the creators negated this fee. These gas fees can be upwards of $200, and since it's an expense, you incur as a result of purchasing an NFT.

Why is this important? Well, when you resell that NFT that you purchased for, let's say, $1000 and sell it for $2000, at first glance, the gain is $1000, right? Yes, but by adding a $200 gas fee to that $1000 original purchase amount means the gains actually only $800 upon reselling it. Unfortunately, most people forget about this and don't factor it into their math when working out capital gains or losses.

- **You can be taxed on airdrops and giveaways.**

Do you remember when Oprah gave away lavished gifts to her audience like cars? Did you know these gifts/giveaways were taxed? Oprah didn't pay the tax on these cars. Her audience who received the cars did. This is the same for NFTs. NFT giveaways are always happening online. They're usually in the form of airdrops where creators share tokens or codes with the 'lucky winners.'

These assets given through airdrops and giveaways are taxed at the average tax rate. However, considering the market's volatility, it's essential to get an accountant to do the work of determining what the correct value of the asset is relative to the value it was before fluctuation.

- **Don't negate the importance of tax planning.**

Taxes and NFTs are not an area where you want to just throw caution to the wind and let whatever happens happen. Instead, before the year ends, determine what your capital gains or losses might be so you can make decisions before it's too late to ease your tax burden.

Key Takeaway

If you're looking to get into this world of NFTs, crypto, and the blockchain, then it's essential to understand the rules and fine print of it all. In addition, you need to know how to prepare for the financial aspects attached to it that aren't mentioned or listed in the price of that NFT you've been looking at. Finally, you also need to understand what potential liabilities exist so that if you're looking to become a digital crypto artist, you don't fall into the legal trap that cuts your career short.

The rules, laws, regulations, perception surrounding NFTs it's all changing. You need to remain aware of these changes. It's so easy for something to fly under the radar, but you don't want to be kept in the dark and learn about it when it's too late.

7

THE DARK SIDE OF NFTS

So we've firmly established that there's a ton of excitement surrounding NFTs. But it shouldn't come as a shock to learn that while there's admittedly a ton of support, excitement, and momentum behind NFTs, they're not without a darker side.

NFTs have never been hailed as the perfect system; it's got problems. Unfortunately, these are problems that even its most die-hard supporters acknowledge. In this chapter, we're going to explore some of these unfortunate downsides attached to NFTs and what disadvantages come with these revolutionary digital assets and the blockchain at large.

These problems range from environmental to security and fraud. It's not all doom and gloom, however. The point is to understand the dark side of NFTs and how you can navigate around or through the problems to find better solutions. So let's take a look at the dark side of NFTs.

NFTs & The Environment

One of the most widely contested aspects of NFTs is their effect on the environment. Climate change has become an issue more commonly discussed in recent years. Most people agree it's time to take it seriously and act accordingly. However, it's hard to ignore NFTs' role in adding to the problem. It's also considered the biggest downside of NFTs. Users want to embrace what is genuinely incredible technology. However, at the same time, they've got to reconcile with the fact that using it is to the planet's detriment.

- **Proof of Stake Algorithms & Their Carbon Footprint**

The Ethereum blockchain, which hosts NFTs, operates on a proof of stake algorithm (PoS algorithm). This algorithm demands an insane amount of computing power in order to verify the transactions being made on the blockchain. It verifies these transactions through various complex calculations, and each transaction ends up using 48.14 kWh per transaction. As a result of requiring so much computing power per transaction, the demand for energy is increased dramatically.

Now it's important to note that if governments took transitioning away from fossil fuels more seriously and actually did something about it, this would be a moot point. But, sadly, we're nowhere near that reality. This means that NFT transactions, of which there are many hundreds of thousands taking place a minute, are adding significantly to the production, burning, and use of fossil fuels to make its very existence possible.

. . .

We have no real way to measure what NFTs are doing to our planet, but it's safe to assume it's not good. NFTs' carbon footprint estimations estimate that a single transaction produces 48 kgs of carbon dioxide. Further research ascertains that one drop of NFT consumes 300kWh, producing 211 kgs of carbon dioxide. Just for reference, that's equivalent to using your computer non-stop for about 10 months.

- **Questions & Disputes**

It's important to note that while NFTs have been continually linked to the adverse effects on our planet, they're far from alone. Some even raise the question of whether they're the main culprit or if they're being used as a scapegoat for miners.

It's uniquely challenging to figure out NFTs culpability when it's such a new technology and when the blockchain as a whole has many areas where these harmful environmental effects are potentially taking place. Most have equated the problem of answering this question to the impossible task of determining your individual share of emissions from a commercial flight. The conundrum raises the question for many that 'if I'm not doing anything, it's still happening regardless.' We've seen this argument used for just about everything when it comes to culpability; the 'one person won't make a difference' argument. This argument ignores the basic concepts of supply and demand. The more individuals take the approach of 'my involvement doesn't make a difference,' the more demand there is in the market as more people engage. The more NFT transactions there are, the higher the value of Ethereum becomes, and that's equal to more miners and machines, ultimately leading to more emissions.

. . .

This system was designed to make these proof of work puzzles progressively difficult. So even if the machines used are more energy-efficient and better at puzzle-solving, they won't be able to keep up with a system designed to facilitate inefficiency.

- **Alternatives**

People are trying to find alternative means to make NFTs greener, and the one way they're doing this is by creating alternatives to proof of work. One of the alternatives that is becoming increasingly popular is 'proof of stake.' This method works by making each user have some skin in the game. To prove you've got skin in the game, you've got to have proof of stake in the form of locked away cryptocurrency tokens in the network. This method has made complex puzzle-solving obsolete and has reduced the emissions produced in the process.

Ethereum has been seeking to make the switch to proof of work for some time now, but they've made no true progress on this front. Furthermore, many doubt Ethereum will ever change as the concerns over tanking the entire system have been floated as a possibility, and nobody is advocating for that outcome.

Another idea being floated is a secondary layer on top of the existing blockchain, which can provide 'off-chain transactions.' This means that traders open their own channels on this secondary layer to engage in unlimited transactions while still having it recorded in the blockchain but in a bundled format. Again, there are existing systems like this, for example, the Lightning Network that launched in 2018.

- **NFTs Going Green**

It's essential to note that while, yes, NFTs have a negative impact on the environment, they're by no means the leading cause of the devastating emissions taking place globally. Artists are leading the charge in making NFTs more environmentally friendly. Some of them are abandoning the home marketplaces and minting their NFTs on networks more sustainable. They're also using marketplaces that accept cleaner cryptocurrencies. It's not an overnight solution, but the discussion is being had. Hopefully, there will be a consensus that helps guide NFTs to greener pastures. Right now, we're not there yet.

NFT Safety & Security

Beyond environmental concerns, there's a dark side to the safety and security NFTs offer. Unfortunately, these downsides have caused issues across mediums, with numerous examples of creator exploitation and stolen likeness being then turned into NFTs, among many other egregious instances of abuse in the NFT space.

- **Theft & Copyright Infringement**

Opportunists are a dime a dozen, and they exist all over the NFT marketplaces. People are constantly taking other artists' work and repackaging it with minor differences before minting and selling an NFT of the asset they stole.

Additionally, some people are taking celebrities' and influencers' identities and turning them into NFTs. SharkTheWeb was at one point a big receiver of backlash for its series of famous influencer NFTs. This has drawn condemnation from those featured in the cards who find them both lazy and unjust. They didn't provide permission, yet their likeness was still used to enrich someone else.

What's most problematic about NFTs is that they've got a strange relationship with copyright laws. While they own the original NFT, there's no protection on copies made of the original NFT. There's nothing you can do to have other people copying your NFT and duplicating it until they're pixelated in the face. You just aren't protected enough, and this affects the marketplace because it allows for frauds and in the worst-case scenario, identity theft. In the most egregious cases, users have taken an artwork of one marketplace and actually uploaded it onto another. This is a true copyright infringement scenario, but now you've got to fight it, and most people give up very quickly, feeling like it's a losing battle.

- **Storage**

At the moment, we've yet to see a blockchain wallet where we can store our NFTs. We currently rely on servers around the world to keep our collections intact. The unfortunate reality means that NFTs aren't as protected by the blockchain if something terrible happens. Hopefully, one day someone will roll out a blockchain wallet. Until then, it's relying on the servers to keep our NFTs safe, even though that's never a guarantee.

- **Scams**

We're so used to scams happening in pretty much every facet of our lives, and while many might assume the blockchain is immune, they'd be sorely mistaken. Here are some of the largest

NFT scams taking place and claiming people's cryptocurrencies daily.

- **Fake NFT Websites**

We've already covered some of the NFT marketplaces out there, but just remember I didn't even mention a quarter of the available options. However, with every legitimate NFT marketplace comes several fakes looking to steal your cryptocurrency. Scammers are seizing on the opportunity of eager, yet naive, investors looking to get in on the action. This lack of awareness ends up resulting in scammers taking your money, or even worse, recording your wallet information such as an address, seed phrase, and more.

Make sure you find the most legit NFT marketplaces available to avoid being caught in the trap. It's also important to implement some browser extensions that pick up alerts notifying you if something about this new site just isn't adding up.

- **Fake Tech Support**

Sometimes you need help, and that's where customer support comes in handy. But, scammers have seized customer support as a means to advance their own efforts to swindle you out of your money and assets. There are two primary ways scammers target NFT enthusiasts. The first is via Discord. Users go online hoping to get some help from the community before being contacted by random people claiming to be employees of different marketplaces. They get you to reveal your information, and it all seems rather benign until you've lost everything. They get your information by requesting you share your screen or redirect you to sites that mirror the marketplace but actually, capture your information. The second way they get people is through email. These emails are usually fake MetaMask security alerts where the threat of your account being frozen looms unless you confirm your details. Once again, everything looks normal until it's too late. The best way to figure out if the emails are legitimate is by checking who sent them and what the redirect link actually is! MetaMask's domain will always be metamask.io. Anything else, close the tab and delete the email immediately.

- **Fake NFT Projects**

This is probably one of the most recently popular scam efforts, and they pop up constantly. New digital tokens are a dime a dozen, they appear almost daily, and people are quick to jump in and buy up these new currencies. Creators of these currencies watch as people buy. The currency peaks before pulling the rug out from under these investors. Of course, the value plummets, and owners aren't able to re-sell. Still, the token's creators are riding high, having just made a profit, often a very healthy profit.

- **Fake Offers**

Scammers like to impersonate as marketplaces and target NFTs you own, claiming somebody has made an offer on one of your NFTs. Then you, unknowingly, click on the button to go to the website. This is where they ask you to link your wallet and seed phrase. The website ultimately captures this information for scammers to infiltrate and pillage your digital wallet.

- **Fake Giveaways**

Who doesn't love a freebie? Nobody, that's the problem. Scammers have been using the giveaway system for decades. They pose as employees of trading platforms and reach out over social media before redirecting you to a website to confirm your identity and claim your prize. But just like with tech support, the links are usually bogus and do nothing but capture your information. If a URL seems dodgy, or if a deal seems too good to be true, then don't be giving away your information to anybody.

- **How to Protect Yourself Against Scams:**

- For starters, always read the URL or email address on communication emails. If the URL or email address looks questionable, which you'll know pretty quickly, then it's best to close the email and delete it immediately.
- Make sure you're using strong passwords and two-factor authentication.
- Consider prices and determine if the number being offered in these emails actually makes sense.
- Verification marks are awarded to legitimate NFT sellers. No verification mark; proceed with caution if you proceed at all.
- Never click on or open attachments unless it's 100% from a reliable source. Unknown sources are never to be entertained.
- Contact customer support through the marketplace website, not in general chat rooms.
- Never share your seed phrase. NEVER. Recovery passwords aren't meant to be shared, just as much as your passwords shouldn't be shared.
- Use the correct tools for storing your money, like legitimate wallet apps.

- **Loss & Disappearance**

The last thing you want to hear is disappearing NFTs but it's true, there are actual cases of NFTs going missing from people's wallets. This can happen for a variety of reasons, such as errors or businesses shuttering and no longer hosting the image. Remember that when you buy an NFT, you're receiving a digital code that directs you to the image or media item. You own the original, which is hosted somewhere in the blockchain. But unfortunately, even on the blockchain, anything can happen.

In September of 2021, OpenSea had a bug, and it caused the destruction and disappearance of 42 NFTs valued collectively at $100,000. Naturally, this raised eyebrows, not just for the people who'd purchased these NFTs but for NFT enthusiasts overall. It raised the question, 'are my NFTs really safe, or am I spending money on something that might completely vanish?'

In the worst-case scenario, a marketplace can close for good, and its hosted assets end up getting deleted, meaning you've lost access to your NFT. Other reasons can include removal due to content that violates the rules, are unreadable, broken, or has been deleted from the source.

Speculations In The NFT Market

NFTs are still largely a misunderstood investment category. Everyone is slowly learning more and more about their potential and their place in the market. But these lingering questions have led to speculations.

- **Pump and dump campaigns**

One of the major speculations being lodged against NFTs is that they're going through a 'pump and dump' campaign. A pump and dump campaign is a manipulative scheme designed to boost stock prices and security by providing fake, often glowing, recommendations.

The recommendations aren't rooted in honest praise. Instead, they use misleading, exaggerated, or downright false claims to back up their claims that these are worthy investments. Many argue that crypto at large is the target of the pump and dump campaigns of the future. Thanks to a lack of regulation, opaqueness, and complexities of the technology, it's very similar to how the Internet boom in the 90s operated. New technology comes along, and while not many people truly understand it, they still want in on the action. They're seeing people getting rich off of it, and they want to be that lucky. Some of them are lucky. Some actually benefit from pump and dump schemes beyond their perpetrators. The majority aren't so lucky, as when it wears off and reality catches up, the value plummets, and investments made become near worthless.

- **Comparisons To Pyramid Schemes**

We throw the term 'pyramid scheme' around a lot, and NFTs are not immune to this. A majority of the people who've invested in NFTs have been extremely high-profile members of society. They're the ones that are making the headlines and bring added relevancy to the platform and concept. They're not the only ones of course, but they're making a splash. They've invested hundreds of millions of dollars in Ethereum, and we've seen a more trickle-down approach as a result.

. . .

Consider the gold rush or the internet boom. Everyone wants to get in on the action, so they buy anything they can pertaining to that market. In the gold rush, everyone bought a shovel, pans, and buckets and went looking for gold. During the internet boom, everyone wanted in on this revolutionary new technology we'd come to know as the internet. People were buying tech stocks and .coms like they were going out of fashion. They were snapping up anything they could. The same goes for NFTs, which still are being snapped up left, right, and center for varying amounts of money in hopes of reselling them after they appreciated value.

The other reason why there's been a comparison to pyramid schemes is that the lion's share of interest in NFTs gets concentrated on a select group of artists while new emerging artists struggle to climb the ranks. This isn't helped by the fact that celebrities and organizations are joining in further saturating the market. In addition, more famous and identifiable artists are joining the digital revolution and bypassing barriers to reign supreme, which has been a source of contention.

While it's somewhat understandable to hear the comparisons, it's not an entirely fair assessment to make. Still, nonetheless, it's a comparison that's been made repeatedly.

- **Unrealistic Evaluations**

One thing that is repeatedly considered when discussing NFTs is that the market is immature and inflated in value. When we take a look at NFTs in terms of liquidity, they don't possess the same qualities as other investments. They're one-of-a-kind assets that can't be replaced, and this complicates things for the buyer. There's no way to get an NFT off their hands quickly and with a healthy return on investment. It takes time. Considering it's extremely difficult to match for buyers and sellers, it's rendered NFTs as ill-liquidity.

Even worse is the volatility of NFTs. Investors want low volatility investments, which means less risk and more potential for strong returns. While yes, NFTs rose 2000% in value over 2020 alone, that's not a great long-term. It's risky growth that puts that immaturity of NFTs on full display. It can take a handful of people pulling out major investments to topple the NFT market in an instance. These have led to many people noting that NFTs are riding a high at the moment. They're new, shiny, interesting, but like the dot.com bubble burst in the 90s, are NFTs on a similar trajectory? This also ties into the considerations that NFTs are experiencing a 'pump and dump' campaign, be it largely intentional or unintentional, nobody is really sure.

We're simply unsure of where the NFT market will land at the end of the day. We're watching in real-time a whole new concept develop before our eyes. While yes, in theory, it could implode. It also has the potential to soar, we just don't really know yet. It makes it both exhilarating and terrifying. That is, however, the nature of investing overall.

Financial Crimes

Beyond the doubts, scams, and risks individual users face with the NFT market, there's another avenue being exploited by high-profile financial criminals who have realized the potential in changing the old ways of moving money and avoiding financial obligations.

- **Money Laundering**

For many in the money laundering space, they've made a discovery, NFTs are perfect for washing dirty money. The days of washing money like Jason Batemen in Ozarks might not be dead, but they've got competition.

Money launderers are now creating and purchasing their own NFTs with dirty money. The blockchain has made this possible thanks to its privacy measures, deregulated digital wallets, and a true misunderstanding of the technology by federal governments.

Now you might be thinking, well at least they're paying taxes on this money, considering NFTs count as capital gains taxes which is roughly a 20% tax. But if you think rich people haven't come up with a way to circumnavigate the tax landscape of NFTs, then you don't know rich people.

- **Tax Evasion**

The lack of visibility that NFT trading provides has provided power to tax evaders who purchase multiple NFTs, give one away that's worth $100,000, and sell another to a friend, relative, or random person for $10,000. As a result, they've just avoided the capital gains tax in a matter of brief transactions.

. . .

Other countries are beginning to realize this, and that's why they're introducing NFT legislation constantly both in Washington and around the world. Even Panama is trying to change how they deal with NFTs. At the same time, marketplaces have already begun testing out new and existing verification measures.

We are already very aware that the US alone fails annually to collect over $1 trillion in taxes every year. With NFTs, this number has all but increased. The IRS has yet to view NFTs as taxable assets. Why? Because they're 'not visible by definition.' While you've got to pay when you take money out, most leave it in the blockchain to continue living on without the payout, all while it continues to make a profit.

Key Takeaway

As it's probably been made clear at this point, while the enthusiasm surrounding NFTs is deserved, it's not all sunshine and rainbows. It's important to remember the context of the situation, and that context is the money. There's an unprecedented amount of money existing in this space right now. Numbers and figures were inconceivable a few years ago, but now the norm. As a result, this lawless land is going to be susceptible to manipulators and con-artists trying to get in on the action in the most illegitimate ways possible.

We've seen this before in things like Wall Street, insider trading, money laundering, and so many other areas where cash is just being thrown into the wind, making it hard to keep track of every transgression. How the blockchain addresses the problem and how they plan on minimizing these effects remains to be seen.

The results, and their efforts, will determine if the blockchain really is a viable future or if we're playing with fire and an untenable entity that's doomed to destroy itself from the inside out. But I'm getting ahead of myself.

Don't let these things deter you from investing and exploring the blockchain. That's not my intention. Instead, my intention is to make you aware of all the risks. The more you know, the better chance you have of navigating around these challenges to secure your future in the digital world.

8

LOOKING INTO THE CRYSTAL BALL

FOR EVERY PERSON enthusiastic about NFTs and the blockchain, there's a bunch of naysayers. Don't take it personally. In the 90s, people also called the internet a fad, and in case you haven't noticed, it was very much not a fad! The thing is, though, NFTs are really new. When the internet was new to the world, nobody was really sure if it would be a permanent fixture in our lives or not. So it's only natural to be in this moment of NFT development where people question if they're here to stay or if they're just an overhyped fad. Who's right? Time will tell.

In this chapter, we will explore the future of NFTs and consider what that will look like and what it tells us about their staying power.

Moving From Experimental To Mainstream

I've made a point to mention a few times that despite NFTs' massive market size, they are not mainstream. There are many people out there who remain entirely in the dark on what an NFT is, let alone the blockchain. There are even people out there with zero knowledge of cryptocurrencies that have been around for over a decade. Progress moves slowly, but NFTs, for the most part, have existed in this experimental stage, now it's beginning to make moves to move towards a more mainstream existence.

According to a Market Analysis conducted in 2021 by Security.org, only 2% of US adults had monetarily interacted with NFTs having either bought or sold them. There's a long way to go until NFTs are mainstream, but a lot is going on that will help to speed up the process.

- **Corporate Interests**

As of 2021, more corporations realize that the world of NFTs offers their business and their brand a great deal of opportunity. It's becoming a movement amongst corporations of all kinds to get involved in this market, selling their own NFTs. As more and more brands get involved, more people will become aware of NFTs. Why? It's simple. While brands benefit from a diversified outreach and revenue stream, NFTs benefit from brands' involvement with built-in customer bases.

The earliest days of 2022 have seen Twitter and Visa getting involved in NFTs. These are just two examples of what is a growing list. This trend is rippling across the business world as more join in the movement. These early decisions made by companies to embrace NFTs affect how other companies decide to approach this foreign market.

- **Celebrity Involvement**

While corporate involvement is undoubtedly boosting the awareness of NFTs and helping legitimize them, nothing has been more potent than celebrity endorsement and involvement. More artists are selling, buying, collecting, and re-selling NFTs.

Celebrities are embracing NFTs far faster than corporations are and have been making headlines with their investments and collections. When these two realities exist, NFTs exposure increases. Increased exposure leads to interest from the general public, who then investigate and attempt to understand this market before ultimately putting their money in play and purchasing NFTs of their own or creating NFTs. The more awareness that exists, the higher the demand becomes over time, which will help bolster NFTs staying power at the end of the day.

Beyond Art

While a small number of the population even knows about NFTs' existence and purpose, most of the people that do know about NFTs are under the impression that it's nothing more than cryptoart. While at the moment, they exist predominantly in a space dominated by digital assets like cryptoart, trading cards, avatars, videos, and other digital assets, experts believe NFTs are going to evolve far beyond their more well-established initial identity.

These estimations go beyond creative means and extend to almost every facet of life.

- **Fleshing Out Digital Identity**

Avatars and profile pictures in the form of NFTs have been among the most successful venture in the world of NFTs. We can easily use CryptoPunks as an example which generated 10,000 NFTs and were all given away for free in 2017. Today, the cheapest CryptoPunk NFT is worth $10,000. At the same time, some fetch in the hundreds of thousands range and, in the most insane examples, sell for millions. There are even celebrities who've snapped up some of these NFT CryptoPunk avatars and use them as their profile pictures on social media. High-profile examples include the likes of Jay-Z, Odell Bechham Jr., Snoop Dogg, and even Visa if you can believe it.

- **Gaming**

The original instance of NFT gaming was the 2017 video game CryptoKitties which allowed users to collect, breed, and then sell or trade their NFT kittens. This was a massive success and even exceeded Ethereum's bottlenecks, ultimately slowing down the entire system.

By 2021, creators had far surpassed CryptoKitties and created hundreds of games centered and built around NFTs. They're even being introduced into existing games. So, where does this go? What's the evolution of NFT games going to be?

The two most prominent examples of NFT gaming exist in the play-to-earn and Metaverse space.

- **Play-to-earn**

Popular examples of play-to-earn games include Axie Infinity and Blankos Block Party. These two examples are being played in mass and making players actual money. It's captured a whole market of people, specifically in low-income or third-world countries.

Axie Infinity is the most popular example of P2E games overall. It was inspired by Pokemon, and it involves players buying, breeding, and training their Axie's characters before sending them into battle or selling/trading them. Players earn the Smooth Love Potion cryptocurrency, which they can sell on secondary markets for traditional money. As it stands, Axie Infinity is considered the most valuable NFT project in the world, with over $1 billion traded on the platform.

- **Metaverse**

Lately, it's hard not to have at least heard of the metaverse. This long-time-coming concept has recently made strides to become a bonafide reality. One of the industries it's shaking up is gaming. Many people believe the Metaverse is the future of online interactions. NFTs are primed to take residency in this digital world that blends virtual and physical reality together.

NFTs will find themselves being used for just about anything in the Metaverse. But they also hold great potential for games in the metaverse, from unique items to art, collectibles, and more.

- **Health & Medical**

The future seeks to make pretty much every part of our lives monetizable. We're seeing that already, but we're moving into a new age where data mining can become consensual and mutually beneficial instead of companies' data mining in secret. But let's focus on health for a moment and how NFTs are changing the medical data world.

In one of the most incredible examples of voluntary medical data collection using NFTs, we turn to Aimedis, a company looking to change the medical data world. Their NFT marketplace allows users to mint their medical data into NFTs to sell to pharmaceutical companies. It's completely optional and mutually beneficial. You get paid, and pharmaceutical companies get data they'd otherwise be lacking or needing to achieve through other more taxing means.

This isn't the only example of medical NFTs making waves, however. Next, we turn to Engin, a Singapore start-up, and their NFT project, 'Health Hero.' This NFT project is seeking to bring health and happiness to a billion-plus people. They're looking to achieve this with NFTs, but not just any NFTs, Well-Being NFTs (W-NFTs). These NFTs are given when you sign up and link them to your tracking devices such as Google Fit, Apple Health, FitBit, etc.

By being healthy and living a healthier lifestyle which includes doing things like exercising, meditating, eating healthy, and adopting healthy habits, you can grow and develop your Well-Being NFT. Developing your W-NFT means making it more unique and rare by adding new characteristics. It's a bizarre concept on its face. Still, there's no denying how intriguing it is and how well it will pay off for the health of billions and financially for Engin.

- **Financial**

One of the most interesting developments in the world of NFTs is the response of the financial world. While many people haven't taken NFTs seriously enough, the financial world has done the complete opposite. Banks now see the value in NFTs and have begun allowing them to be used as collateral for loans. This allows investors to gain back liquidity without risking or sacrificing their ownership. It's almost like a mortgage where you're leveraging your digital asset to create liquidity.

This is just the beginning of the financial world's relationship with NFTs, as many have made predictions that NFTs could solve long-standing issues of financing long supply chains. More banks and financial institutions will get involved in NFTs, as made evident by Visa's recent entry into the market where they bought a CryptoPink NFT. Even venture capital firms are taking an intense interest and focus on NFTs projects and just in Web 3.0 in general.

- **Real-World Utility Tokens**

NFTs have already begun being used to represent real-world utilities, services, benefits, and products. A great example of this is event tickets. Mark Cuban, a big NFT advocate and investor, plans to bring NFT tickets to the NBA. Kings of Leon have sold NFT lifetime tickets to fans, so they always have front-row seats for their tours.

. . .

Beyond tickets, NFTs are also being used as proof of ownership, to manage licenses, and so much more.

New NFT Developments

New developments in the world of NFTs are happening every day, so it shouldn't surprise anyone how much is actually going on in this space. Here are some of the emerging developments that can tell us a lot about where the world of NFTs is heading as it continues to become more mainstream.

- **NFT Fragments**

NFT fragments are essentially making NFTs similar to that of stocks. The effort is to take high-value NFTs and make them more liquid and accessible by fragmenting them so more people can own a part of an expensive NFT. This can be any number of pieces like a few chunks or a million shards. This makes it far more accessible for people who aren't able to get in on major NFT purchases right out of the gate. It's also great if you want to be in on purchasing a piece of historic NFTs.

Famous examples of fragmented NFTs include the infamous Doge meme, which was fragmented by its original owner and allowed investors to own a slice of history for as little as a dollar. Another example is Picasso's art, which was offered to investors in 4000 fragments.

- **Entertainment**

Everyone is getting into streaming these days, so why not NFTs? Creators are selling NFTs with digital content attached like episodes of a show and giving access to consumers by letting them join a community as a result of their purchase. A famous example of this is The Stoner Cats. High-quality actors such as Mila Kunis, Jane Fonda, Chirs Rock, Seth MacFarlane, and even the creator of Ethereum, Vitallik Buterin, have made this dream a reality.

Other companies realize they need to break into this space to avoid getting left behind. Film companies like Warner Bros, Fox, Disney, and other big hitters are putting aside millions to explore the possibilities of the blockchain across all its many facets. It's not long before we've got a whole new streaming service on our hands that truly breaks the mold. It's going to be incredible to witness this unfold.

What makes this aspect of NFTs interesting is community engagement. Imagine saying things in a community that influences the creators of this content. NFTs are essentially democratizing countless industries, and everyone is taking an 'if you can't beat em,' join em.'

- **Twin NFTs**

Digital Twin NFTs are basically NFTs of a physical product or asset. This will allow for digital records of ownership of physical assets. What this will do for the world is aid in reducing trade and sale of fake goods. In addition, we'd be able to have the firmest means of authentication necessary. As items gain digital records that are immune to manipulation and counterfeiting thanks to the blockchain, which makes altering records impossible, we reduce the power counterfeiters have over the markets.

You'd never be left wondering if your items are fakes because you'll have the records to prove their authenticity. It will make the resale market more honest and less exploitative, with well-produced counterfeits being sold every day to people assuming they're getting a legit product. These records will be stored in your wallet, so there's never any doubt of authenticity.

Some companies are already doing this, such as Nike, which launched CryptoKickcs, a blockchain verification system for their shoes. Some companies are partnering with blockchain firms to tokenize ownership records, such as Prada, LVMH, and Cartier. This is only set to continue as more companies realize the value in shutting down counterfeiting efforts.

- **AI NFTs**

AI NFTs are becoming a thing recently, with AI-generated art being a massive trend in the community. AI art is remarkable because it's created and minted entirely by AI. These AI artists study art by famous artists or art of specific genres/time periods. Then the AI makes something from those references. One of the earliest examples is an AI artwork from 2018, which fetched $400,000.

Another example of AI in the NFT space is the existence of iNFTs. These specific types of NFTs are given AI personalities.

These personalities are equipped to hold a conversation, learn new things, and change their personality as they live and exist on the blockchain. Alice, an example of an iNFT, sold for half a million dollars, and the company behind her, Alethea AI, is working on a metaverse of their own called Noah's Ark. The company plans to have the capacity for owners to train their iNFTs and eventually have them earn money in the Metaverse.

It seems crazy that this is where the NFT space is heading, and in some ways already has, but it just echos everything we've already come to know about NFTs: they're revolutionary. The power of the people will determine the success of the show existing only on the blockchain.

New Rights of Ownership Opportunities

A major shake-up NFTs are facilitating is rights of ownership opportunities.

- **Photography**

Photographers and their art stand to benefit from NFTs, which could offer a stronger sense of ownership and copyright control that current systems don't offer, or at least protect, enough. Right now, prominent examples of sites/services photographers use to monetize their work include the likes of Shutterstock or iStockPhoto, among others. Unfortunately, they're not great as there are many instances of them violating the copyright. Beyond that, there's an issue with redistribution and a lack of ability to authenticate licensed work.

. . .

NFTs offer a strong shift and change to an outdated and inadequate system. Photographers take back the power to mint their work and sell licenses to photos as NFT fragments. This means that proving ownership is easy, thanks to digital wallets. Additionally, photographers are getting paid adequately for their work, considering they'll be determining the price they deem most fair. This even better benefits license holders as they can transfer licenses if they no longer need them. It provides greater control for artists and freedom for users. It also has the potential to be a lot cheaper, considering no middle man is facilitating the sale and licensing.

- **Music**

Incredibly interesting and currently underutilized if utilized at all, music licensing stands to benefit immensely from using NFTs. When streaming rendered CDs obsolete, we lost a part of music that's been felt since those discs stopped spinning, and that's the idea of collectability in music. While vinyl has made a comeback, it's safe to say CDs likely won't. The proposal is that artists and labels release musicians' past albums as NFTs, which offers another streaming avenue. Buyers can sell the album, trade it, or continue owning it and watching as it increases in value as the band or the album grows in popularity. There's a way to make an album an event this way by tying albums to additional elements like concerts, meet and greets, and other exclusivities that add value. The most significant benefit of this is the fan interactions with the band or singer. It takes the fan experience to a whole new level.

- **Ownership Transfers**

NFTs also have the power to change how we transfer ownership, which is either impossible or highly challenging for many things.

- **Real Estate**

Our current methods of transferring property ownership are costly and complicated. NFTs offer an alternative that makes transferring ownership far easier. The way it works is that NFTs are created for a property, which is then bought or leased (rentals); when it comes time to sell or rent, the token is transferred to a buyer or renter. The other potential avenue for using NFTs on properties is co-owning and treating homes as investments meaning you own a fraction of the home, but everything is well documented. So it not only becomes cheaper, but it also becomes far more efficient.

- **Textbooks & Other Works**

College textbooks have long been the bane of students' existence. They're excessive in price, and this leads students to purchase physical copies and then resell them after their course ends. Unfortunately, buying a digital textbook means they can't resell it once they're done, and that's where NFTs come in!

Turning a textbook into an NFT means that students can resell the textbook once they no longer need it. Universities have yet to go down this path, but it's a path that makes a lot of sense. As it stands, when a textbook is sold second-hand, they get nothing on that sale. That's how second-hand works, but if that textbook was an NFT, they'd get money on every sale. So not only could they make more money, but the students would also be able to get some of the money back on the book they no longer need. It's one of the most incredible examples of a win-win situation.

Developments That Are Boosting NFTs Relevance

Significant developments are happening in the blockchain arena, boosting NFTs relevancy and giving some insight into how they fit into the forthcoming digital age. Those three things are the crypto economy, eco-friendly blockchain developments, and the Metaverse.

- **Crypto Economy**

When the internet came about in the 90s, businesses began adapting to a new way of operating. A more connected environment focused on data sharing, collaboration, more accessible communication, and logistics. As a result, the economy as a whole transformed and has been continuing to transform over the years.

We're now in a new age, where the world is slowly adopting a crypto economy. Everything we currently know is changing. The speeds at which things are changing are different depending on the sector and designation. We're seeing the creative industry embracing the blockchain far quicker than almost any other industry. This is the gateway to the full-fledged crypto-economy dream many people have had for years.

As more businesses and industries find interesting ways, they can adopt the blockchain into their business process the more we inch closer to that reality. It's not just about businesses. It's also about entire industries and governments doing the same.

. . .

I've mentioned before that healthcare is becoming more and more blockchain-focused in recent years. This is just one industry, but they're far from alone. Logistics, shipping, and supply chains are exploring the use of blockchain to increase transparency and efficiency. Even local governments are looking at better ways to manage citizen information. More and more people are acknowledging the power of blockchain and how NFTs might be the answer to more than just the world of art, collectibles, and creative endeavors. One can't really exist without the other. As much as the blockchain will be needed to achieve these goals that companies have to improve their processes, they'll need NFTs to implement these objectives effectively.

- **Eco-Friendly NFTs & Crypto**

It's long been known that many elements on the blockchain aren't necessarily the greenest technologies in the world. In fact, they're far from it. Some cryptocurrencies are absolute gas guzzlers. This has given the entire technology a truly awful environmental record and reputation, as we discussed in Chapter 7.

Moves are being made to change a lot of things to create a more green and sustainable blockchain. How? Well, it's not necessarily a simple task. See, it's a matter of establishing guidelines that users of the blockchain can adopt to reduce the overall carbon footprint. Let's look at a few examples of what is being proposed:

- **Lazy Minting** = To lazy mint is to only mint an NFT as it's been purchased for the first time. It's not a dramatic improvement on the current process, but it is about 2 or 3x less carbon footprint overall.

- **Sidechains** = The concept of sidechains allows creators to mint NFTs on other non-Ethereum based PoS and allow for moving to Ethereum later.
- **Bridges** = Making blockchain ecosystems compatible and allowing them to interact. The primary advantage of this is allowing you to go from ETH to another less impactful chain without losing your already minted data.
- **Various Layer 2 (L2) Scaling Optimizations** = up to 100x more efficient than the current system.

These are the recommendations as they relate to Ethereum. Other blockchains have already been developed that are far less gas-intensive and are far better on the environment than Ethereum is its current form.

Even in terms of cryptocurrencies, some currencies are far less harmful to the environment than others. Popular cryptocurrency Bitcoin is well known to be devastating on carbon emissions. While other coins such as Cardano, Hedera, and Nano as good examples of cryptocurrencies with a less substantial carbon footprint.

The problem is the adoption of these alternatives. They need to be adopted by a majority of blockchain users to make a difference, and that's where the problem lies. Ethereum is the most popular blockchain as it stands. While it has room for change and improvement, it's yet to take any steps towards a greener existence. Time will tell where they eventually land on the matter, especially as public pressure builds.

- **Metaverse**

The talks surrounding widespread adoption and interaction with metaverses is increasing daily. A metaverse is a persistent digital space or spaces. It's where the physical and virtual worlds collide, and people and brands can interact in a digital world. There are already some metaverses that exist, such as Decentraland, which was built on top of Ethereum and has built-in support for NFTs already. This, however, is only the beginning of what the metaverse is and plans to be in the near future.

As more people embrace the metaverse, we see the potential for NFTs to become a prominent feature of these digital environments and worlds. For example, displaying NFT art, having NFT deeds, NFT avatars, blockchain gaming, and metaverse asset, which are purchasable NFTs. The possibilities indeed are endless, and it's evident it will be the law of the virtual land.

Key Takeaway

NFTs are creeping their way into just about everything. While the adoption of this new emerging technology is slow-moving for the most part, the more people that get involved, the greater the momentum ends up being. Right now, NFTs' most crucial use case is in the art and collectible world. But, as other industries use and embrace it, its influence only grows stronger.

For years, many people have been actively avoiding and ignoring the noise of NFTs. Assuming they'd be a passing fad or a young man's game meant people put their heads in the sand. Now, it might be time to acknowledge that we've got little to no option when it comes to learning about this new world that's shaping before our eyes. There may come a time when NFT and blockchain ignorance leads to technological illiteracy.

The future of NFTs is bright. For better or worse, it's going to change the world. So we've got to decide how we will approach this new world and the many changes that are coming our way.

CONCLUSION

Well, we're at the end of our journey into the blockchain. Together we've gone through a lot of what the blockchain is all about. While NFTs are what our focus was, we realized that the blockchain has a lot of uses, many of which remain untapped.

Now that you've gotten through this intensive eight chapter guide to the world of NFTs, the blockchain, crypto, and beyond, it's time to start investing. I realize that reading about it and doing it are two different things. As a result, you might feel nervous about what lies ahead. However, as I stated many times through the eight chapters, sometimes you've got to take risks to experience the rewards.

Over the years, I've experienced both success and failure in the NFT game. While it sucks when you lose, you learn to not make the same mistakes twice. I think the most important lesson I can part with is that in order to succeed with NFTs, you need to be adaptable. This is a fast-moving world and market that changes rapidly day-to-day. You need to know what's going on and how to adapt to these changes on the go.

You know all about the blockchain, how crypto and NFTs came to be, how to buy, sell, transact, trade, and the fine print. You also know that NFTs aren't perfect, and they've got their downsides while also having an incredibly bright future. You should be leaving this book feeling empowered and ready to try your hand at this emerging market. Whether you're creating, collecting, or both, it's time to seize this moment! There is no need to wait any longer. It's time to act. Continue learning, but learn from doing as much as you do from books, articles, and community engagement. Always keep the advice and guidance in mind and refer back whenever you need it. I'll be right here on these pages reminding you all about the path forward.

You've got the tools, you've got the knowledge, now it is time to go out and put it all to the test! Good luck. I can't wait to see you succeed!

9

RESOURCES

Beattie, A. (2022, January 30). Contemplating Collectible Investments. Investopedia. https://www.investopedia.com/articles/basics/06/contemplatingcollectibles.asp

Investing in collectibles: 5 types of collectibles that have historically offered bankable returns. (2021, February 24). Business Insider. https://www.businessinsider.com/collectible-investments-valuable-types?IR=T

Chen, J. (2022, February 3). Investing in Collectibles. Investopedia. https://www.investopedia.com/terms/c/collectible.asp

B. (n.d.). CryptoKitties | Market History and sales trends. NonFungible.Com. https://nonfungible.com/market/history/cryptokitties?filter=saleType%3D&length=10&sort=blockTimestamp%3Ddesc&start=999990

. . .

Statista. (2022, January 11). Daily sales and price of NFT collection CryptoPunks to January 10, 2022. https://www.statista.com/statistics/1265555/cryptopunks-nft-development/

Adams, R. C. (2021, December 30). 30 NFT Statistics to Understand in 2022 [Market, Sales & Trends]. Young and the Invested. https://youngandtheinvested.com/nft-statistics/

Hong, S., & Hong, S. (2022b, January 5). 9 celebrities who have entered the NFT world, from Leo Messi to Justin Bieber. Lifestyle Asia Hong Kong. https://www.lifestyleasia.com/hk/culture/the-arts/celebrity-nfts-cryptocurrency-metaverse/

Chapter 1

Conti, R. (2022, February 15). *What Is An NFT? Non-Fungible Tokens Explained.* Forbes Advisor. https://www.forbes.com/advisor/investing/nft-non-fungible-token/

Alexiades, H. (2021, November 30). *Where do NFTs actually come from? A short history of non-fungible tokens*. Alternative Press Magazine. https://www.altpress.com/meta/history-of-nfts-non-funfible-tokens/

P. (2022, February 9). *The History of NFTs & How They Got Started.* Portion Blog. https://blog.portion.io/the-history-of-nfts-how-they-got-started/

Steinwold, A. (2021, December 12). *The History of Non-Fungible Tokens (NFTs) - Andrew Steinwold.* Medium. https://

medium.com/@Andrew.Steinwold/the-history-of-non-fungible-tokens-nfts-f362ca57ae10

Putnam Investments. (n.d.). *Behind the NFT hype: Answers to five common questions*. https://www.putnam.com/individual/content/advisorTechTips/3444-behind-the-nft-hype-answers-to-five-common-questions

Conti, R. (2022b, February 15). *What Is An NFT? Non-Fungible Tokens Explained*. Forbes Advisor. https://www.forbes.com/advisor/investing/nft-non-fungible-token/

NFT 101 Collecting guide to 'non-fungible tokens.' (2022, February 2). Christies. https://www.christies.com/features/NFT-101-Collection-Guide-to-NFT-11654-7.aspx

Geroni, D. (2021, September 1). *The Advantages of Non-Fungible Tokens (NFTs)*. 101 Blockchains. https://101blockchains.com/advantages-of-nfts/

Kramer, M. D. P. (2022, January 18). *Beginner's Guide to NFTs: What Are Non-Fungible Tokens?* Decrypt. https://decrypt.co/resources/non-fungible-tokens-nfts-explained-guide-learn-blockchain

Fungibility: When Interchangeability Matters. (2021, January 24). Investopedia. https://www.investopedia.com/terms/f/fungibility.asp#:%7E:text=Key%20Takeaways-,Fungibility%20is%20the%20ability%20of%20a%20good%20or%20asset%20to,houses%2C%20are%20non%2Dfungible.

White-Gomez, A. (n.d.). *Are NFTs Only Art? 7 Use Cases For NFTs*. One37Pm. https://www.one37pm.com/nft/tech/are-nfts-only-art-use-cases-for-nfts

Geroni, D. (2021, September 3). *Understanding the Different Types of NFTs*. 101 Blockchains. https://101blockchains.com/types-of-non-fungible-tokens/

Non-Fungible Token (NFT). (2022, February 26). Investopedia. https://www.investopedia.com/non-fungible-tokens-nft-5115211

Rancea, B. (2021, October 11). *What Gives NFT Value?* Ecommerce Platforms. https://ecommerce-platforms.com/cryptocurrency/what-gives-nft-value

Chang, H. (2021, December 13). *Understanding the value of Non-Fungible Tokens (NFT)*. Medium. https://medium.com/@changhugo/understanding-the-value-of-non-fungible-tokens-nft-49d2713bdfc4

Chapter 2

Silver, N. S. (2021, December 10). *The History And Future Of NFTs*. Forbes. https://www.forbes.com/sites/nicolesilver/2021/11/02/the-history-and-future-of-nfts/?sh=5960f06d6a16

Conway, L. (2021, September 22). *What Is a Blockchain? The Simple Explanation*. The Street Crypto: Bitcoin and Cryptocurrency News, Advice, Analysis and More. https://www.thestreet.com/crypto/bitcoin/what-is-a-blockchain-the-simple-explanation

BuiltIn. (n.d.). *What Is Blockchain Technology? How Does It Work?* Built In. https://builtin.com/blockchain

Dutta, A. (2021, July 23). *Real-World Applications of Blockchain Technologies*. Analytics Insight. https://www.analyticsinsight.net/real-world-applications-of-blockchain-technologies/

Daley, S. (2021, December 16). *34 Blockchain Applications and Real-World Use Cases Disrupting the Status Quo*. Built In. https://builtin.com/blockchain/blockchain-applications

CoinMarketCap. (n.d.). *Cryptocurrency Prices, Charts And Market Capitalizations*. https://coinmarketcap.com/

Hayes, A. (2022, February 14). *10 Important Cryptocurrencies Other Than Bitcoin*. Investopedia. https://www.investopedia.com/tech/most-important-cryptocurrencies-other-than-bitcoin/#:%7E:text=One%20reason%20for%20this%20is,communities%20of%20backers%20and%20investors.

Gemini. (n.d.). Public and Private Keys: What Are They? https://www.gemini.com/cryptopedia/public-private-keys-cryptography#section-what-is-a-private-key

Visual Editor. (2021, September 22). *The Basics Of NFTs: Digital Art & Collectibles on the Blockchain*. Expensivity. https://www.expensivity.com/what-is-an-nft/

NDTV Business Desk. (2021, September 1). *What Is The Difference Between NFTs, Cryptocurrency And Digital Currency?* NDTV.Com. https://www.ndtv.com/business/nfts-cryptocurrency-and-digital-currency-how-do-they-stack-up-against-each-other-2525054

Conti, R. (2021, May 24). *What Is An NFT? Non-Fungible Tokens Explained*. Forbes Advisor UK. https://www.forbes.com/uk/advisor/investing/nft-non-fungible-token/

Williams, S. (2018, January 3). *Cryptocurrencies Explained, in Plain English*. The Motley Fool. https://www.fool.com/investing/2018/01/02/cryptocurrencies-explained-in-plain-english.aspx

Ethereum. (n.d.). *ERC-721 Non-Fungible Token Standard*. Ethereum.Org. https://ethereum.org/en/developers/docs/standards/tokens/erc-721/#:%7E:text=The%20ERC%2D721%20(Ethereum%20Request,for%20tokens%20within%20Smart%20Contracts.

NextAdvisor. (2021, August 12). *Ethereum: What You Should Know Before You Invest.* NextAdvisor with TIME. https://time.com/nextadvisor/investing/cryptocurrency/what-is-ethereum/

Zafar, T. (2021, December 22). *Blockchain, NFTs, and the New Standard for Identity and Security.* Entrepreneur. https://www.entrepreneur.com/article/403417

Chapter 3

I. (2021c, September 8). *Cryptoart: digital art and NFTs | Connections by Finsa.* Connections By Finsa. https://www.connectionsbyfinsa.com/what-is-cryptoart/?lang=en

What Is Crypto Art And How Does It Work? (n.d.). Eden Gallery. https://www.eden-gallery.com/news/what-is-crypto-art

D. (2022c, January 6). *Digital Art vs. NFTs: Understanding the Difference - Del'art.* Medium. https://delart-co.medium.com/digital-art-vs-nfts-bc7a6762a4f3

How do NFTs solve the problem of digital artwork ownership? (n.d.). CTriartd. https://www.ctrlartd.com/post/how-do-nfts-solve-the-problem-of-digital-artwork-ownership

BBC News. (2021, September 23). *What are NFTs and why are some worth millions?* https://www.bbc.com/news/technology-56371912

Hertzmann, A. (2021, March 15). *Why would anyone buy crypto art – let alone spend millions on what's essentially a link to a JPEG file?* The Conversation. https://theconversation.com/why-would-anyone-buy-crypto-art-let-alone-spend-millions-on-whats-essentially-a-link-to-a-jpeg-file-157115

A. (2021a, March 11). *To Buy or Not To Buy CryptoArt.* Aaron Hertzmann's Blog. https://aaronhertzmann.com/2021/03/11/cryptoart.html

McLaughlin, R. (2021, December 21). *'I went from having to borrow money to making $4m in a day': how NFTs are shaking up the art world.* The Guardian. https://www.theguardian.com/artanddesign/2021/nov/06/how-nfts-non-fungible-tokens-are-shaking-up-the-art-world

Locke, T. (2022, January 19). *Billionaire investor Mark Cuban says this is the moment that "really got me into" crypto.* CNBC. https://www.cnbc.com/2022/01/19/billionaire-mark-cuban-on-why-nfts-led-him-to-be-a-crypto-evangelist.html

Gray, J. (2021, March 9). *These celebrities are bringing NFTs to the mainstream — and cashing in.* The Business of Business. https://www.businessofbusiness.com/articles/nft-celebrity-non-fungible-tokens-crypto-grimes-paris-hilton/

Dobrik, J. (2022, March 7). *Is NFT art a good investment? Understand why people buy digital art.* ValiantCEO. https://valiantceo.com/is-nft-art-a-good-investment/

Rooney, K. (2021, December 4). *Crypto investors see looming NFT bubble but tout staying power of the underlying tech.* CNBC. https://www.cnbc.com/2021/12/03/crypto-investors-see-an-nft-bubble-but-tout-power-of-underlying-tech.html

Chapter 4

Yeung, T. (2021, March 11). *Want to Become a Millionaire on NFTs? Do it the Right Way.* InvestorPlace. https://investorplace.com/2021/03/want-to-become-a-millionaire-on-nfts/

How To Invest in NFTs. (2022, January 6). The Balance. https://www.thebalance.com/how-to-invest-in-nfts-5215020

Christine, A. (2021, March 17). *Why Should I Buy #CryptoArt?* Alissa Christine. https://www.alissachristine.love/blog/2020/10/why-should-i-buy-crypto-art

We talked to crypto-art investors to figure out what's driving people to spend millions on NFTs, despite no guarantee their value will increase. (2021, May 11). Business Insider. https://www.businessinsider.com/why-are-people-buying-nfts-investing-in-nft-crypto-art-2021-3?international=true&r=US&IR=T

Conti, R. (2021, May 24). *What Is An NFT? Non-Fungible Tokens Explained.* Forbes Advisor UK. https://www.forbes.com/uk/advisor/investing/nft-non-fungible-token/

Staff, T. A. (2022, March 9). *Best NFT Wallets*. The Motley Fool. https://www.fool.com/the-ascent/cryptocurrency/best-nft-wallets/

S. (2022c, January 4). *How to Choose an NFT Marketplace in 2022 - SpaceSeven*. Medium. https://medium.com/space-seven/how-to-choose-an-nft-marketplace-in-2022-4bf671c3647d

A. (2022b, March 12). *Securely Storing Your NFTs: A Complete Guide*. Cyber Scrilla. https://cyberscrilla.com/securely-storing-your-nfts-a-complete-guide/

How To Secure NFTs? (2022, February 2). Ledger. https://www.ledger.com/academy/how-to-secure-your-nfts

Ahmad, W., & Security, V. C. (2022, January 28). *How to Secure, Back Up, and Protect NFTs*. Vault12. https://vault12.com/securemycrypto/crypto-security-basics/nft-security/particle-18

McDonald, L. (2021, July 29). *Diversifying Your Portfolio: How NFTs May Fit Into Your Financial Strategy*. Sarson Funds | Cryptocurrency & Blockchain Investment Funds. https://www.

sarsonfunds.com/diversifying-your-portfolio-how-nfts-may-fit-into-your-financial-strategy/

Investing in NFTs: Why It Matters. (2021, May 25). Portfolio for the Future | CAIA. https://caia.org/blog/2021/05/25/investing-in-nfts-why-it-matters

Sophy, J. (2022, March 3). *How to Make Money with NFT*. Small Business Trends. https://smallbiztrends.com/2022/01/nft.html

Defiance ETFs. (2022, March 4). *How to Invest in NFT Stocks: The Best Options for 2022*. https://www.defianceetfs.com/6-nft-stocks-for-2022/

Chapter 5

Locke, T. (2021, May 13). *These millennial creators are making 6 figures selling NFTs: "It changed the trajectory of my career and my life."* CNBC. https://www.cnbc.com/2021/05/12/meet-the-millennial-creators-making-six-figures-selling-nfts.html

Street, N. (2021a, November 12). *How to Monetize Your NFT's? The Complete Guide*. NFT's Street. https://www.nftsstreet.com/how-to-monetize-your-nfts/

Arney, J. (2022, January 15). *How To Make Money With NFTs*. Expensivity. https://www.expensivity.com/how-to-make-money-with-nfts/

Sergeenkov, A. (2021, December 11). *5 Ways to Earn Passive Income From NFTs*. Coindesk. https://www.coindesk.com/learn/5-ways-to-earn-passive-income-from-nfts/

Sant, H. (2022, February 21). *Non-Fungible Tokens (NFTs) and Their Applications in Other Fields*. Geekflare. https://geekflare.com/finance/nft-creation-and-applications/

Author, G. (2022, March 11). *How to Create and Sell NFTs for Free*. PetaPixel. https://petapixel.com/how-to-create-sell-nfts-for-free/

Sturdevant, S. (2022, January 7). *Pricing Strategy for Artists: 8 Keys to List Your NFTs for Success | by Sophie Sturdevant | Apr, 2021 |*. Medium. https://sophiesturdevant.medium.com/pricing-strategy-for-artists-7-keys-to-list-your-nfts-for-success-fefe00ed4ef0

How to Promote your NFT Collection: Free and Paid Ways. (n.d.). NFT Calendar. https://nftcalendar.io/nft101/promote-nft-collection/

Siu, E. (2022, January 19). *How to Promote Your NFTs the Right Way*. Single Grain. https://www.singlegrain.com/web3/how-to-promote-nfts/

Chapter 6

What are the legal issues around NFTs? | Osborne Clarke. (n.d.). Osborne Clark. https://www.osborneclarke.com/insights/what-are-legal-issues-around-nfts

C. (2021a, October 7). *9 Legal Issues That Stand Behind NFTs | OpenGeeksLab*. Web And Mobile Apps Development, UI/UX Design | OpenGeeksLab. https://opengeekslab.com/blog/legal-issues-nfts/

The Rise of NFTs – Opportunities and Legal Issues. (2021, April 20). White & Case LLP International Law Firm, Global Law Practice. https://www.whitecase.com/publications/alert/rise-nfts-opportunities-and-legal-issues

NFTs and the Right of Publicity: Assessing the Legal Risks. (n.d.). JD Supra. https://www.jdsupra.com/legalnews/nfts-and-the-right-of-publicity-9050692/

Hwang, B. (2021, November 2). *The developing legal landscape of NFTs*. Lexology. https://www.lexology.com/library/detail.aspx?g=47d2d377-6233-41ba-b2fe-23814cd3a456

NFT Tax Guide: What Creators and Investors Need to Know About NFT Taxes. (n.d.). TaxBit Blog. https://taxbit.com/blog/nft-tax-guide-what-creators-and-investors-need-to-know-about-nft-taxes/

Chapter 7

Calma, J. (2021, March 15). *The climate controversy swirling around NFTs*. The Verge. https://www.theverge.com/2021/3/15/22328203/nft-cryptoart-ethereum-blockchain-climate-change

Non-Fungible Tokens (NFTs) Explained | AWS Blockchain. (n.d.). Amazon Web Services, Inc. https://aws.amazon.com/blockchain/nfts-explained/

Street, N. (2021, November 12). *The Dark Side of NFT's and Crypto Art*. NFT's Street. https://www.nftsstreet.com/the-dark-side-of-nfts-and-crypto-art/

J. (2021b, June 9). *Is NFT a Good Investment To Add To Your Portfolio?* Los Angeles Angel Investor and Venture Capital Partner- Jonathan Hung. https://jonathanhung.com/are-nfts-a-good-investment/

Dean, I. (2022, January 18). *The dark side of NFTs ignites controversy among gaming YouTubers*. Creative Bloq. https://www.creativebloq.com/news/nfts-ignite-controversy-amongst-gaming-youtubers

DeMatteo, M. (2022, January 18). *NFT Scams: How to Avoid Falling Victim*. CoinDesk. https://www.coindesk.com/learn/nft-scams-how-to-avoid-falling-victim/

A. (2022a, January 4). *Dark side of NFTs: money laundering and more.* Medium. https://alfacash.medium.com/dark-side-of-nfts-scams-money-laundering-and-pollution-46b8971a3892

Munster, B. (2021, March 29). *People's Expensive NFTs Keep Vanishing. This Is Why.* Vice. https://www.vice.com/en/article/pkdj79/peoples-expensive-nfts-keep-vanishing-this-is-why

Brahambhatt, R. (2021, November 3). *NFTs Are Mysteriously Disappearing, Here's How.* Interesting Engineering. https://interestingengineering.com/nfts-are-mysteriously-disappearing-heres-how

Sier, J. (2021, September 27). *Why some NFTs are valuable and others aren't.* Australian Financial Review. https://www.afr.com/technology/why-some-nfts-are-valuable-and-others-aren-t-20210917-p58sld

The Dark Side of NFTs. (2021, March 21). The Big Idea. https://www.thebigidea.nz/stories/the-dark-side-of-nfts

M, S. (2021, December 13). *The Dark Side Of NFT.* Jumpstart Magazine. https://www.jumpstartmag.com/the-dark-side-of-nft/

Chapter 8

Queue-it. (2022, January 26). *11 exciting NFT trends shaping the future of non-fungible tokens*. https://queue-it.com/blog/exciting-future-nft-trends/

Dossett, J. (2022, January 1). *5 predictions for bitcoin, NFTs, and the future of money*. CNET. https://www.cnet.com/personal-finance/crypto/5-predictions-for-bitcoin-nfts-and-the-future-of-money/

Morse, J. (2021, December 21). *Sick of NFTs? Insiders insist they're just getting started.* Mashable SEA. https://sea.mashable.

com/tech/18700/sick-of-nfts-insiders-insist-theyre-just-getting-started

Boscovic, D. (2021, March 31). *How nonfungible tokens work and where they get their value – a cryptocurrency expert explains NFTs*. The Conversation. https://theconversation.com/how-nonfungible-tokens-work-and-where-they-get-their-value-a-cryptocurrency-expert-explains-nfts-157489

Schwartz, M. (2021, May 26). *Beyond Beeple's $69M NFT: How creators can (and will) thrive in the crypto economy*. Fast Company. https://www.fastcompany.com/90637977/beyond-beeples-69m-nft-how-creators-can-and-will-thrive-in-the-crypto-economy

I. (2021, June 17). *A Guide to Ecofriendly CryptoArt (NFTs)*. Branch. https://branch.climateaction.tech/issues/issue-2/a-guide-to-ecofriendly-cryptoart-nfts/

P. (2022, March 3). *The History of NFTs & How They Got Started*. Portion Blog. https://blog.portion.io/the-history-of-nfts-how-they-got-started/

Made in the USA
Las Vegas, NV
07 May 2022